# EXPLORE THE WORLD

# PRAGUE

*Authors:*
*Bernd F. Gruschwitz, Hans-Horst Skupy,*
*Kerstin und André Micklitza*

*An Up-to-date travel guide*
*with 53 color photos*
*and 9 maps*

# NELLES

# LEGEND / IMPRINT

**Dear Reader:** Being up-to-date is the main goal of the Nelles series. Our correspondents help keep us abreast of the latest developments in the travel scene, while our cartographers see to it that maps are also kept completely current. However, as the travel world is constantly changing, we cannot guarantee that all the information contained in our books is always valid. Should you come across a discrepancy, please contact us at: Nelles Verlag, Schleissheimer Str. 371 b, 80935 Munich, Germany; Tel: (089) 3571940; Fax: (089) 35719430; e-mail: Nelles.Verlag@t-online.de

**Note:** Distances and measurements, including temperatures, used in this guide are metric. For conversion information, please see the *Guidelines* section of this book.

## LEGEND

| | | |
|---|---|---|
| ★★ ★★ | Main Attraction *(on map)* *(in text)* | ✝ Church |
| ★ ★ | Worth Seeing *(on map)* *(in text)* | ✡ Synagogue |
| ❽ | Orientation Number in Text and on Map | ℹ Tourist Information |
| ■ | Public or Significant Building | ☎ Post Office |
| ■ | Hotel | † Cemetery |
| P | Parking | ▲ Campsite |

Pedestrian Zone

U Müstek — Underground

Railway

🅢🅢🅢 Luxury Hotel Category
🅢🅢 Moderate Hotel Category
🅢 Budget Hotel Category

*(for price information see "Accomodation" in Guidlines section)*

## PRAGUE

© Nelles Verlag GmbH, 80935 München
  All rights reserved
  First Edition 2001

ISBN 3-88618-235-5 (Nelles Travel Pack)
ISBN 3-88618-861-2 (Nelles Pocket)
Printed in Slovenia

| | | | |
|---|---|---|---|
| **Publisher:** | Günter Nelles | **Translation:** | Sidaway Sollinger / Transwords |
| **Project Editor:** | Bernd F. Gruschwitz | | |
| **Editor-in-Chief:** | Berthold Schwarz | **Photo Editor:** | K. Bärmann-Thümmel |
| **Editor:** | Sylvi Zähle | **Color Separation:** | Priegnitz, München |
| **English Editor:** | Sidaway Sollinger / Transwords | **Cartography:** | Nelles Verlag |
| | | **Printed by:** | Gorenjski Tisk |

                                                                                        - S03 -

# TABLE OF CONTENTS

## TRAVEL INFORMATION

## MAP LIST

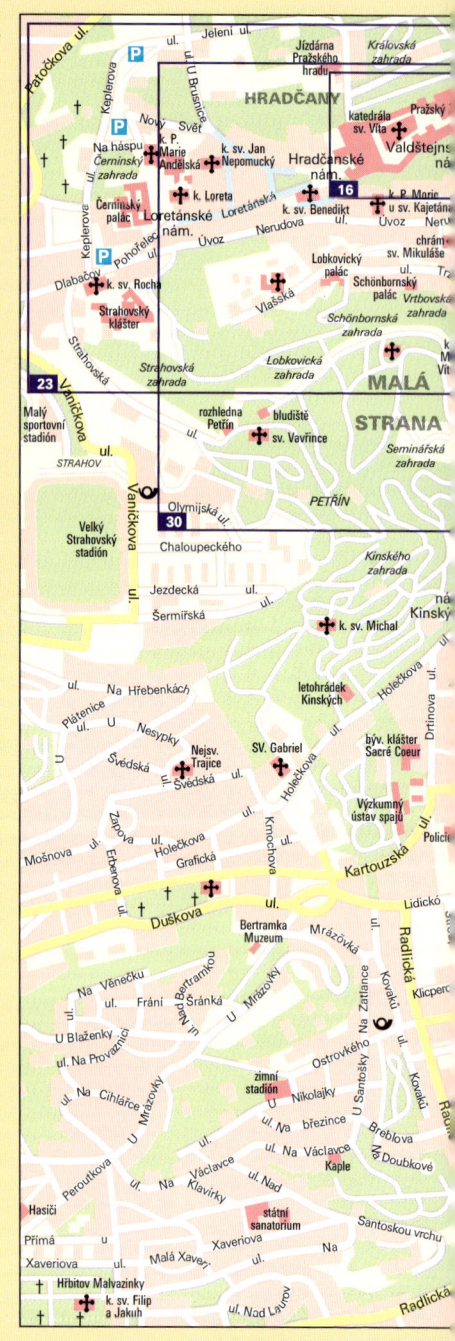

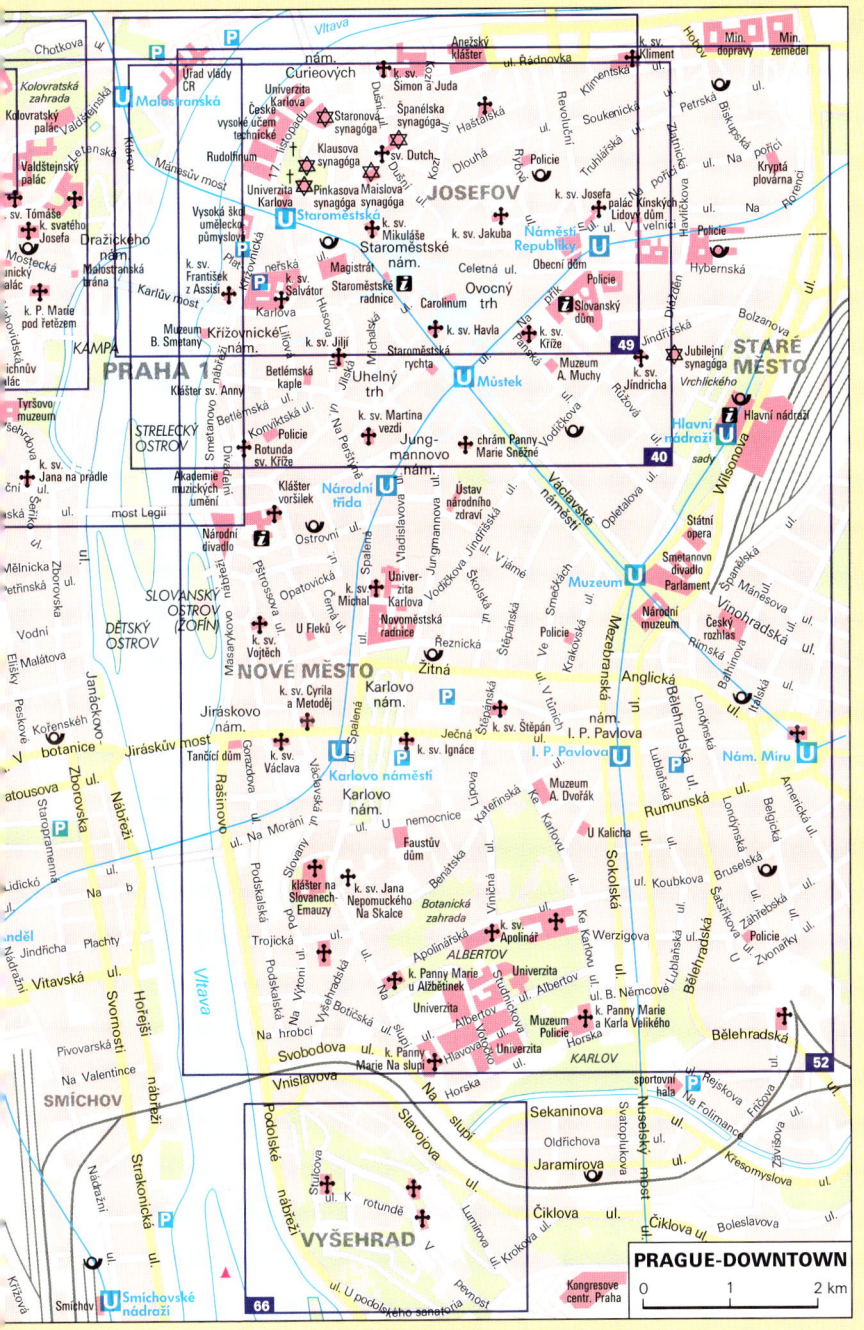

**PRAGUE-DOWNTOWN**

0          1          2 km

## The Beginnings

**500 to 100 B.C.** Slavic tribes settle in what are now the regions of Bohemia and Moravia. In the **9th century** the Great Moravian Empire, forerunner of Czechoslovakia, consolidates. From **863** missionary activities of the "Slavic apostles" Cyril and Methodius; they develop a Slavic script. In **908** Magyars destroy the Moravian Empire.

## The Premyslid Dynasty and the Golden Epoch

**995** In the struggle for power in Bohemia, the Premyslid family dynasty emerges as the victor.

**10th / 11th centuries** The Premyslid monarchs secure their power with the help of the Roman Empire. Bohemia becomes a fiefdom of Germany.

**1212** Ottokar (Otakar) II attracts German settlers to the border areas of Bohemia.

**1306** The Premyslid dynasty dies out.

**1310** Elizabeth (Eliška), daughter of the Bohemian King Wenceslas (Václav) III, marries John of Luxemburg. John is granted Bohemia as fiefdom.

**1316-1378** Charles IV, son of Elizabeth and John, becomes the German King and Emperor. Bohemia flourishes during this period. Prague is the capital of the Holy Roman Empire. The "states of the Bohemian crown" encompass Bohemia, Moravia, the Silesian duchies and Upper and Lower Lusatia.

## The Hussite Movement

**1414** The preacher and rector Jan Hus, who calls for reform in the Church and a renunciation of its worldly power, is burned at the stake as a heretic.

**1419** The Hussite Wars under the leadership of Jan Žižka make Catholic Europe tremble.

**1436** King and Council confirm the Hussite confession as an autonomous constituent of the Roman church. The Pope does not accept this situation. Bohemia remains a region of religious struggle.

**1471** The Bohemian crown is handed over to the Polish Jagellon dynasty.

**1526** The Bohemian state parliament chooses Hapsburger Archduke Ferdinand as the King of Bohemia. Ferdinand supports the Counter Reformation.

**1547** Ferdinand I campaigns against the Schmalkaldic League. Bohemian nobles refuse to recognize him. Ferdinand moves against Prague: nobles lose their privileges; possessions and income are confiscated.

## The Thirty Years' War

**1618** The "Defenestration of Prague" triggers the Thirty Years' War. The Bohemian Diet declares Ferdinand II deposed.

**1620/1621** Czech Estates defeated on White Mountain near Prague. Hapsburgs execute the leaders of the rebellion. End of Bohemian independent state.

## Bohemia under the Hapsburgs

**1627** Bohemia fully incorporated into the Hapsburg Empire. Catholic faith imposed on all. Tens of thou-

*Jan Hus at the stake (wood carving 1558).*

sands flee, seeking religious freedom. Population reduced by one third; economy in shambles.

**18th century** Relations improve following reforms by monarchs Maria Theresa (1740-1780) and Joseph II. (1780-1790): compulsory education, end of serfdom, justice system reform, abolition of torture and death penalty, policy of religious tolerance.

## The First Republic of Czechoslovakia

**1848** Czech people call for a federalist state.

**1918** Establishment of the Republic of Czechoslovakia on October 28. Thomas G. Masaryk is the President, Edvard Beneš is Foreign Minister.

**The 1920's** Initially, reconciliation of the German minority with the new state. The Republic of Czechoslovakia (ČSR) is one of the world's ten leading industrial states, but is caught in the grip of the global economic depression in 1929.

**1930-1932** Exacerbation of the conflict among nationalities.

**1933** Konrad Henlein founds the "Sudetendeutsche Heimatfront" (from 1935 Sudetendeutsche Party). At

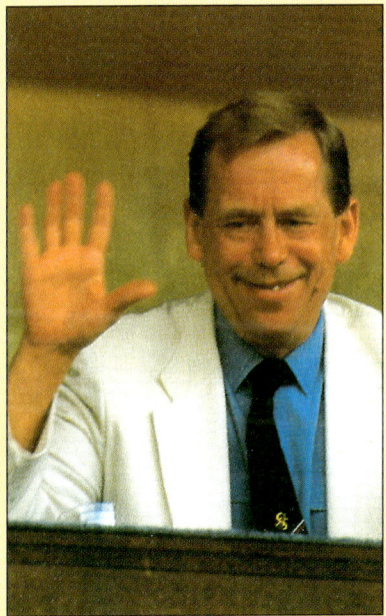

*Czech President Václav Havel.*

first they call for an autonomous administration within the republic, then the annexation to Hitler's Germany.

### Czechoslovakia during the Second World War

**1938** 90 % of the German population of Czechoslovakia vote for the Sudetendeutsche Party. On September 29, heads of state of England, France, Italy and Germany meet in Munich; the border (Sudeten) areas settled by Germans are ceded to Germany. President Beneš emigrates to England.

**March 15, 1939** Annexation of the rest of Czechoslovakia by Germany.

**1942** Attempted assassination by a Czech paratrooper of German Reich Governor, Heydrich; avenged by the destruction of the village Lidice and mass shootings. During the occupation, some 200,000 Jews are transported through the Theresienstadt Concentration Camp to the gas chambers.

**1945** Americans liberate western Bohemia, May 5. The Soviet army enters Prague on May 9. President-in-exile Beneš returns.

### Post-War Years and "Prague Spring"

**1946/1947** Expulsion of ca. 3.6 million Germans, tens of thousands lose their lives. The Communists win the elections; Klement Gottwald becomes Communist Party chief.

**1948** Gottwald succeeds Beneš as President. Farms are forcibly collectivized, industries nationalized, opponents of the regime persecuted.

**1962** Process of de-Stalinization. Alexander Dubček is named Chairman of the Slovakian Communist Party.

**1968** Movement to reform state and economy. A spread of reformist ideas and activity is feared in "brotherlands." On August 21, the ČSSR is occupied by armies of the Warsaw Pact. Reform politicians removed from power. Thirty thousand Czechs and Slovaks leave their homeland.

**1970's** The economy stagnates. After the CSCE Conference, 257 citizens sign the "Charta 77" for the preservation of human rights. The regime reacts with arrests and persecutions.

### From the Velvet Revolution to Today

**November 1989** The suppression of a student demonstration in Prague in November 1989 sets off the "Velvet Revolution." Within three weeks, the Communist government resigns. Václav Havel is elected President of the country on December 29.

**January 1, 1993** Dissolution of Czechoslovakia into the Czech Republic and the Republic of Slovakia, from this point on, independent republics.

**1995** The Czech Republic becomes a member of the OECD, the alliance of the leading industrial nations of the world.

**1999** Czech Republic joins NATO.

## PRAGUE – GOLDEN CITY IN THE HEART OF EUROPE

For many, it is love at first sight, for Prague is magnificent, full of splendor and charm. This city has an indescribable attraction, especially for artists and those interested in art. Richard Wagner was delighted with Prague; Humboldt even described it as the loveliest city in Europe. Poets have long sung the city's praises; and ever since the 15th century, painters have captured its panorama, the picturesque views and the grandeur of its edifices. It is still a center for poets, painters, composers and film-makers.

Prague is often described as "the secret capital of Europe," and it is graced with many other sonorous names: "Golden Prague" on account of the legendary

*Previous pages: Little Night Music. Marionettes in front of St. Nicholas Church in the Old Town. Above: Bridge over the Vtlava. Right: The Czech national dish vepřo – knedlo – zelo (roast pork, dumplings and cabbage).*

splendor, which accumulated in Medieval times. "Prague of the Hundred Towers" actually has 473 towers. The numerous houses of worship and cloisters have made Prague "The Rome of the North." Due reverence for the rhythmic magnificence of the entire work of art which is Prague is demonstrated by the nickname, "Petrified Symphony." "Magical Prague" relates to the mystical legend of Dr. Faust and of the artificially created Golem. And it is said that Prague is the "City of Dreams."

Prague is addictive. One can return again and again and yet not even begin to see everything. Over 30 million visitors per year are enchanted by the city's charm. Most visitors climb to the the old royal town of Hradčany, saunter through the Lesser Town and around the Old Town Ring. They visit noble palaces, churches, cloisters, and, of course, the Castle of Hradčany, or Prague Castle, which towers over the historical city center. It is considered to be the archetype for various artistic styles and trends.

From the Old Town's Bridge Tower on Charles Bridge one looks down on an army of ants: thousands of tourists walking up to Prague Castle on the world-famous bridge. It is only very early in the morning that one has the possibility of being alone on the Charles Bridge, observed only by the sculptures of the saints.

A varied museum landscape, music, theater and film festivals, art exhibits and concerts attract thousands to its orbit. And one tradition has been maintained: Mozart, Weber, Beethoven, Wagner, Liszt, Smetana and Dvořák celebrated great success in Prague. The range of museums, theatrical events and concerts is overwhelming – and for the visitor to Prague it is easy and simple to find one's way around, for throughout the streets of the Old Town there are many clear signs pointing the way to cultural venues. Be it the Community Hall, the Rudolfinum, Black Mountain, Clam-Gallas or the Lobkowitz Palace in the Hradčany district – many historical buildings form an impressive background for first-class cultural enjoyment.

The world's youth also adores Prague. Everywhere in the city on the Vtlava River one meets young people, especially Americans: some 20,000 to 30,000 of them live here, and many opt to remain for several years.

Prague owes much of its attraction to the Bohemian King Charles IV, who is considered the founder of Prague's Gothic structures. Following his rise as Holy Roman Emperor, Prague became for a time the capital of the Holy Roman Empire of German Nations. The university, the New Town and Lesser Town, St Vitus' Cathedral and the Charles Bridge were founded. The former "City of Three Cultures" – Czechoslovakian, German and Jewish – has experienced a great deal. Times of harmony and peace alternated with times of strife and torment. The greatest tragedy occurred during the Sec-

*Discovering Prague*

ond World War: Prague's Jews were murdered in Nazi extermination camps. Following the war, most of Prague's Germans were forced to leave the city. Now the Czechs were among themselves, but they were not free: there followed the hated partnership with the Soviet Union. For over four decades, the "life nerves" of the city to the West were cut off. But in 1989, times changed in Prague when poet and dissident Václav Havel moved into the Castle as State President. Following this political turning point, the historical center was lovingly restored.

Prague's very cobblestones echo with history, wherever one goes. They are, however, quite hard on the feet, and one's legs tire easily. But there are numerous cafes, restaurants and pubs which invite the visitor for a rest. The delicious aromas of dumplings and freshly-drawn beer waft through the air. Oases for rest, relaxation and falling in love can be found in the quiet parks and gardens, in the twisty little streets and on small, romantic squares.

# EXPERIENCING PRAGUE

**CASTLE / HRADČANY**
**LESSER TOWN**
**OLD TOWN**
**JOSEFOV**
**NEW TOWN**

## THE **HRADČANY AND ITS **CASTLE

Standing watch high over the city on the Vtlava is **Prague Castle** ❶ (*Pražský hrad*). Constructed in the 9th century, the castle began as a wooden fortress surrounded by earthen bulwarks, and was gradually transformed to assume the imposing form it has today, an appearance it took on during the reign of Maria Theresa in the 18th century. "I see a ship; its mast is Hradčany...," wrote the poet Vítězslav Nezval (1900-1958).

Prague Castle stands as a symbol of worldly power. Counts and margraves, princes and kings, emperors and presidents have governed Bohemia from this fortress. In all the world, there is no older ruling house still accomplishing its original task. Throughout its history, Prague Castle has served not only as the seat of the secular government, but also as a religious center, as evidenced by St. Vitus Cathedral and its chapels, or the museum-like St. George's Basilica. Most of the palaces on the castle grounds now house museums with important artistic treasures. About three dozen secular and sacred historical sites located within Prague

*Left: Window by Alfons Mucha in St.Vitus Cathedral.*

Castle make this the country's most important cultural monument. Numerous guests from all over the world daily visit the area around the castle. The little shops on Golden Lane (*Zlatá ulička*) bustle with thriving, and sometimes dubious, commercial activity. A visit to Prague Castle takes at least half a day, excluding the museums.

### First Castle Courtyard

The ideal starting point is the **First Castle Courtyard** ❶, which can be reached by way of Castle Square (*Hradčanské náměstí*). Viennese court architect Niccolò Pacassi designed the Court of Honor, as the First Castle Courtyard is also known. The entrance with its magnificent iron grille gate, flanked by two sentries from the castle guard, is adorned with two oversized statues of fighting giants (copies). The original statues were designed in 1769 by Ignaz Platzer the Elder, who also designed the vases and figures around the top of the palace and on the so-called **Matthew Gate** (*Matyášova brána*). The allegorical figures above the gate represent war and peace. The sandstone gate itself was carved in honor of King Matthew around 1614. The coat-of-arms symbolizes the countries which, at that time, were part of the Hapsburg Em-

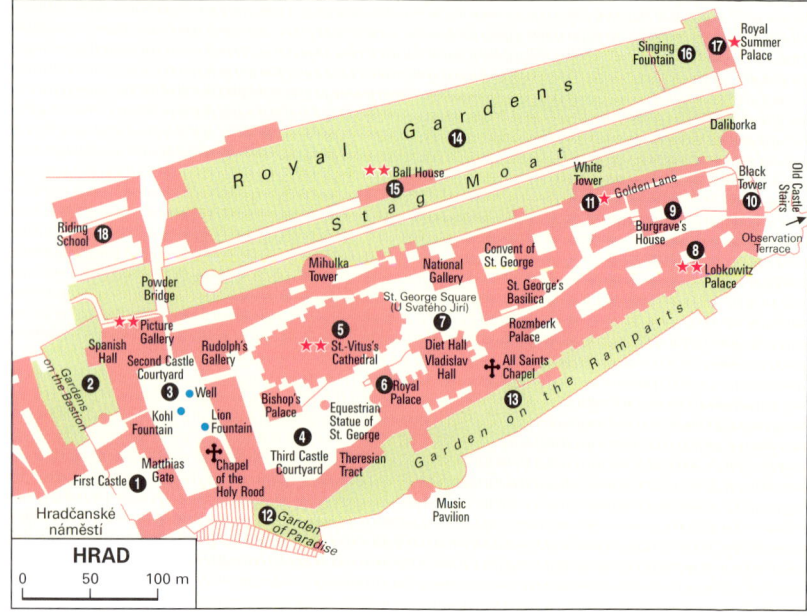

pire. When the flag waves above the presidential wing, the Czech president is in residence. The changing of the guard takes place every hour on the hour, from 5:00 a.m. to 11:00 p.m.; at noon, there's a ceremonial parade as the new guards march in to take up their duties and the old ones retreat. A small gate leads to the **bastion gardens** ❷ (*Zahrada Na baště*).

### Second Castle Courtyard and **Picture Gallery

Commissioned by Maria Theresa, Pacassi also created the **Second Castle Courtyard** ❸ by filling in the castle moat. Some of the rooms in the surrounding buildings have been converted for state purposes, and are no longer open to the public. Among these are the legendary Rudolph's Gallery with its elaborate stucco work, and the huge Spanish Hall, 48 meters long, 24 meters wide and 12

*Right: View from the Lesser Town of Prague Castle and St. Vitus Cathedral.*

meters high, an unforgettable setting for concerts held here from June to October. Two fountains and a well are found in the second courtyard: the lion fountain from 1967, the Baroque bubbling fountain from 1686, and the draw-well with its handcrafted wrought-iron grille (1702).

The **Picture Gallery** (*Obrazárna Pražského hradu*) forms the north side; this building once housed the magnificent imperial carriages. But the exhibits on display are only fragments of what was once a phenomenal collection of paintings assembled during the reign of Emperor Rudolph II (1575-1611) in the middle of the 17th century, which was later scattered far and wide. Nevertheless, the gallery attempts to present an exhibit of Renaissance art, supplemented by Baroque and Rococo elements. Among the prominent Italian artists represented here are Jacopo and Francesco Bassano, Titian, Jacopo and Domenico Tintoretto, as well as Paolo Veronese. A monumental painting by Peter Paul Rubens, *Meeting of the Olympian Gods*, is in Room IV.

Castle / Hradčany

Paintings by Peter Brandl and portraits by Jan Kupetzky demonstrate the local variant of High Baroque. Statues created in Bohemia by Matthias Braun glorify Prague's golden age.

The **Chapel of the Holy Cross** (*Kaple svatého Kříže*) was designed in the second half of the 18th century by Anselmo Lurago; the decorative figures on the high and side altars are the work of Ignaz Platzer. The wall and ceiling paintings are the joint effort of Josef Navrátil and W. Kandler, the central painting on the high altar is the work of court painter Franz Xaver Palko. The chapel houses Prague Castle's information center (April-Oct., daily 9:00 a.m. to 4:00 p.m., www.hrad.cz). The cathedral's treasures – relics, shrines, busts, crucifixes, vestments, monstrances, bibles, paintings, plaques, jewels, the helmet and chainmail shirt of St. Wenceslas, as well as St. Stephen's sword – are no longer on display here. These devotional objects will be shown on the Gothic floor of the Royal Palace.

**The Third Castle Courtyard and **St. Vitus Cathedral**

After the founding of the Czechoslovakian Republic in 1918, archaeologists began excavating within the castle walls. In the **Third Castle Courtyard ❹**, they uncovered early medieval earthen bulwarks as well as fragments of Romanesque and Gothic buildings. Dominating not only the Third Courtyard but the entire city is ****St. Vitus Cathedral ❺** (*chrám svatého Víta*). Most amateur photographers are perplexed when they gaze through their viewer, for it seems impossible to take a picture of the entire cathedral. In fact, it can only be achieved using an extremely wide-angle camera lens. The main steeple with its four Renaissance bells is Prague's highest tower, measuring exactly 99.6 meters. The triple-naved church is 124 meters in length, and has a transept which is 60 meters wide and 33 meters high. 28 pillars support the vaulting. The rose window above the west portal measures 10.4 meters in

diameter. The cathedral was a silent witness to the coronations and funerals of the long succession of Bohemian kings. King Charles IV had this Gothic church built on the site of a former Romanesque basilica. After the death in 1352 of the first architect, Mathieu d'Arras, the cathedral was completed by the German architect, Peter Parler, and his sons around 1420. A Renaissance dome was added to the main steeple in 1554, which was converted to a Baroque onion-dome in 1770. The busts in the triforium, including those of Charles IV and his four wives, and of Mathieu d'Arras and Peter Parler, date from the 14th century. The high altar and several of the 21 chapels display neo-Gothic traits (built 1868-1875).

In the southern part of the transept, the Gothic cathedral chapel, better known as **\*\*St. Wenceslas Chapel** *(Kaple svatého*

*Above: The famous St. Wenceslas Chapel in St. Vitus Cathedral. Right: The "Defenestration of Prague" in the Bohemian Chancellery. Painting by Václav Brožík, 1889.*

*Václava)*, attracts masses of visitors. Wenceslas is deemed Bohemia's patron saint. The chapel was built by Peter Parler between1362 and1364. In addition to the magnificent Passion cycle by an anonymous 14th-century master, are the inlays of more than 1,300 semiprecious stones: amethyst, agate and jasper stones were pressed into the wet plaster. Just as in a fairy tale, the **crown jewels** – the Wenceslas crown, studded with sapphires, emeralds and crystal, from 1346; the Imperial orb and scepter; and the golden sword – are sealed in a treasury with seven locks and seven keys. Each key is safeguarded by one of seven different state institutions, so that access to this priceless treasure is a joint venture in the most literal sense. This, the country's second most important cultural treasure, is only displayed on important state holidays during leap years. Johann Fischer von Erlach designed the Baroque silver **tomb of St. John Nepomucene** in the chapel. B. Wohlmuth created the Renaissance style **organ loft**. The **art nouveau**

**glass windows** by famous local artists (A. Mucha, M. Švabinský, K. Svolinský, etc) are interesting.

Above the **Golden Portal** on the south side of the cathedral is a restored Bohemian glass mosaic of *The Last Judgment* from around 1370, during the reign of Charles IV. The equestrian statue of St. George, created by the brothers Georg and Martin of Klausenburg (Cluj, Romania), also dates from this epoch. A copy can be found in the courtyard; the original statue is on display in St. George's Monastery. The **Royal Crypt** contains the coffin of Charles IV as well as those of many other rulers (though some are merely symbolic). Nestled up against the cathedral is the old **bishop's residence**, which received a Baroque facade in the 17th century. Located in the Third Castle Courtyard is the entrance to the office of President Václav Havel.

In the former **Royal Palace ❻** (*Královský palác*), which served as the residence until well into the 16th century, the so-called Bohemian Chancellery was the seat of the Hapsburg governors. It was here in 1618 that three imperial civil servants were thrown from the window by an angry mob; this was the start of the Thirty Year's War. All three victims survived their 16-meter descent, spared by a dungheap which broke their fall. One of the castle's most impressive rooms is the magnificent **Vladislav Hall** (*Vladislavský sál*), built by Benedikt Ried between 1486 and 1502. It is 62 meters long, 16 meters wide and 13 meters high and bears the name of the Bohemian King Vladislav of the Polish Jagiello dynasty. It is here that the head of state takes the oath of office.

The Czech Parliament meets in the *Stará Sněmovna*, the **Old Diet Hall**, built between 1559-61 by B. Wohlmuth. Leading up to Vladislav Hall, the huge stairway with its late Gothic rib vaulting is truly impressive. Here, too, is All Saints Chapel, built by Peter Parler (1370-1387) and rebuilt after a fire in 1541. The All Saints painting on the high altar was created by W. L. Reiner. Chris-

tian Dittmann painted (1669), the dozen scenes from the life of the Bohemian medieval national patron, Prokop, on the choir walls. The **Mihulka Tower** behind St. Vitus' Cathedral, a part of the fortress dating from the 15th century, is now used for exhibitions. On display is an original alchemist's laboratory.

### St. George's Square and *Golden Lane

A few steps further is **St. George's Square** ❼ (*U svatého Jiří*), and **St. George's Basilica**, one of the oldest structures on the castle grounds – or, for that matter, in the whole city. Although this twin-towered church was built in the middle of the 12th century, a much smaller one stood on this site 200 years earlier. Today's basilica, which appears Romanesque, is the result of restoration done between 1897-1907. The early Re-

*Above: St. George's Basilica. Right: Tiny craftsmen's houses in Golden Lane.*

naissance portal stems from the workshop of Benedikt Ried; the Baroque facade adornments were added in 1678. František Maximilian Kaňka added the Nepomucene chapel to the basilica between 1718 and 1722; the chapel's frescoes and altarpiece are by Wenzel Lorenz Reiner; while its statue of the Nepomucene was created by Ferdinand Maximilian Brokoff, one of the sculptors responsible for Charles Bridge. The Chapel of St. Ludmilla dates from the 13th and 14th centuries; the frescoes in the Renaissance vaulting are 16th century.

The **Benedictine Convent of St. George** *(Kláster svatého Jiří)* was the first Bohemian convent for women. Mlada, Prince Boleslav II's sister, founded the convent in the year 973. In 1782, it was secularized by Joseph II; thereafter, it was occasionally used as a barracks. Since 1974, Bohemian art works from the Gothic period to the Baroque have been exhibited here, as well as early Gothic panel paintings and the medieval Madonnas. During the 16th century, one of the most important Bohemian aristocratic families, the Lobkowitz family, purchased in 1651 the magnificent **★★Lobkowitz Palace ❽** (*Lobkovický palác*, in the Jiřská), built in 1570 by Vratislav de Pernštejn. It serves today as a branch of the National Museum.

Since the 16th century, the former **Burgrave's House ❾** has served a variety of functions. This Renaissance structure has been used as a law court, a residence, and, from 1963, as the "House of Czechoslovakian Children." Today, there is a toy museum here. Not far away is the **Black Tower ❿** (*Černá věž*), whose small platform provides a lovely panorama. The other two towers, also the remains of the former fortifications, are the **White Tower** (*Bílá věž*) and the **Daliborka** (featured in Smetana's opera, *Dalibor*). The latter was built by Benedikt Ried towards the end of the 15th century. Until 1781, the tower served as a dungeon. The history of its first prisoner and namesake, Dalibor von Kozojedy, was made famous through Smetana's opera.

Do not descend from the castle via the **Old Castle Stairs** (*Staré zámecké schody*), for you will miss a major attraction: **★Golden Lane ⓫**, *Zlatá ulička*. The tiny houses were built directly against the castle wall at the end of the 16th century, in which the castle archers and gatekeepers set up little craftsmen's establishments. Today, they harbor flourishing souvenir shops. In 1917-1918, Franz Kafka found his inspiration in what then was certainly a more peaceful environment in house No. 22.

### Gardens and Museums

The castle is surrounded on several sides by well-tended gardens that have only recently been opened to the public. These lovely oases of tranquility are just the thing for relaxing after a sightseeing tour. The **Paradise Gardens ⓬** (*Rajská zahrada*) were documented as early as the

*Castle / Hradčany*

16th century, while the **Garden on the Ramparts ⓭** (*Zahrada Na valech*) was laid out in the 19th century. The most expansive public park, the 16th-century **Royal Gardens ⓮** (*Královská zahrada*), contains three buildings with landmark statues. The sgraffito-covered **★★Ball House ⓯** (*Míčovna*), built by Bonifatius Wohlmuth 1567-69, houses Flemish Gobelin tapestries from the 17th century. The **Singing Fountains ⓰** (*Zpívající fontána*) were also created during this period by Tomáš Jaroš. The Italian architect Paolo della Stella designed the magnificent **★Royal Summer Palace ⓱** (*Letohrádek*), also known as **Belvedere**, for Anna Jagiellonska, wife of the Hapsburg Emperor Ferdinand I. This Renaissance structure, with its delicate arcades was completed in 1563 by Wohlmuth.

The former **Riding School ⓲** (*Jízdárna*) has housed a gallery for 20th-century Czech art since the end of the 1940s. It was built at the end of the 17th century by Jean B. Mathey, an architect who was active throughout Bohemia. The **Powder**

Bridge (*Prašný most*) leads over the former **Stag Moat** (*Jelení příkop*), which served as a barrier between the gardens and the royal game preserve.

### A Walk Through **Hradčany

The castle is the crowning glory of the **Hradčany district, which nestles closely to the edifice. In 1598, Hradčany became Prague's fourth independent city. In addition to numerous churches, it is dominated by the splendid palaces of wealthy aristocrats from the 16th and 17th centuries. The square *Hradčanské náměstí ❷ is surrounded by more than half a dozen magnificent structures. The sgrafitto-adorned Renaissance **Schwarzenberg Palace**, (No. 2) on the south side of the square now houses the **Museum of Military History**. On display are weapons and tools of war from over eight centuries and from every corner of Europe.

*Above: An up-to-date reflection of a Prague city palace (Tuscany Palace).*

The **Tuscany Palace** (*Toskánský palác*), an early Baroque edifice built in 1690 by Jean B. Mathey, now belongs to the Foreign Ministry. Before 1694, this Burgundian architect had also remodeled the **Archbishop's Palace** (*Arcibiskupský palác*) to the north; the Rococo facade was added (J.J. Wirch) in 1764-65. Every year, on the Thursday before Lent, the Cardinal opens to the public a few of the sumptuously-decorated rooms, resplendent with paintings, tapestries, Gobelins and porcelain dating from several centuries, as well as frescoes and plaster-work.

The near-by **Martinitz Palace** (*Martinický palác*) is closely linked with the name of Governor Martinitz, who was unceremoniously thrown out of the castle window onto a pile of manure in 1618. Today, concerts are held in the palace's grand hall. Slightly hidden behind the Archbishop's Palace is the **Sternberg Palace ❸ (*Šternberský palác*), which is the seat of the administration of the splendid fine arts collection of the **National Gallery** (cf page 70). In this splendid pal-

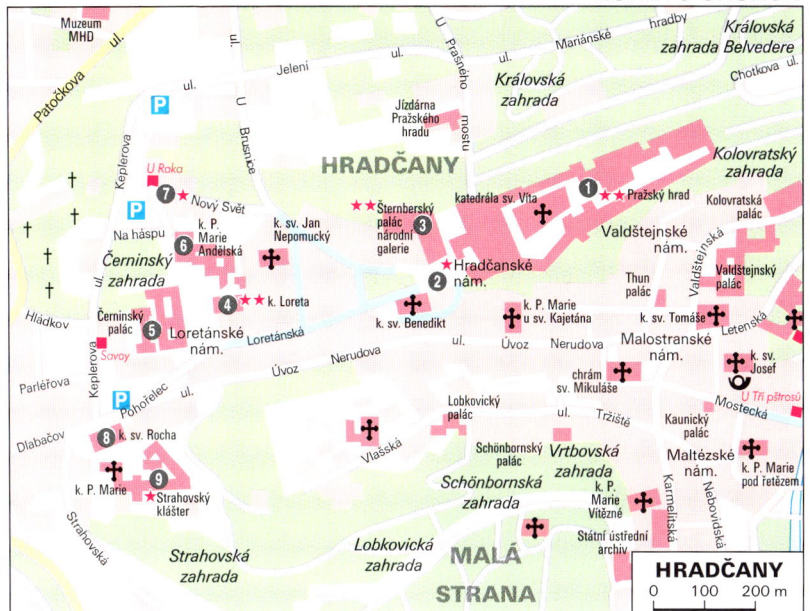

Map labels: Muzeum MHD, Patočkova ul., Keplerova, U Raka, Nový Svět, Na háspu, Černínský zahrada, Hládkov, Černínský palác, Parléřova, Pohořelec ul., Dlabačov, k. sv. Rocha, k. P. Marie, Strahovský klášter, Strahovská, Strahovská zahrada, k. P. Marie, Andělská, k. sv. Jan Nepomucký, Šternberský palác, národní galerie, k. Loreta, Loretánské nám., Loretánská, Úvoz, Vlašská, Schönbornský palác, Schönbornská zahrada, Lobkovická zahrada, Jízdárna Pražského hradu, Jeleni, Pražského mostu, Králová zahrada, katedrála sv. Víta, Hradčanské nám., k. sv. Benedikt, Nerudova, Mariánské, hradby, Pražský hrad, Valdštejnské nám., Thun palác, k. P. Marie u sv. Kajetána, Malostranské nám., chrám sv. Mikuláše, Lobkovický palác, Tržišté, Vrtbovská zahrada, k. P. Marie Vítězné, Státní ústřední archiv, MALÁ STRANA, Královská zahrada Belvedere, Chotkova ul., Kolovratský zahrada, Kolovratská palác, Valdštejnský palác, Letenská, k. sv. Tomáše, k. sv. Josef, U Tří pštrosů, Mostecká, Kaunický palác, Maltézské nám., k. P. Marie pod řetězem, Nebovidská, Karmelitská. **HRADČANY** 0 100 200 m

Castle / Hradčany

ace, built by Alliprandi and Martinelli from 1698 to 1720, is a collection of international works. In addition to some 400,000 graphic works and drawings, the National Gallery has some 14,000 paintings and over 6,000 sculptures; among these are 8,000 works of Oriental art. The National Gallery's collections are world-renowned, even though after the advent of democracy in 1990 some works had to be given back to their rightful owners. One of the collection's strengths is Italian art of the 14th to 18th centuries; also notable are the German and Dutch paintings of the 15th and 16th centuries, 16th- and 17th-century Flemish paintings, and French art from the last two centuries. From the terrace of the castle square there is a lovely view across the spires and rooftops of the Lesser Town, the Old Town and the New Town, all the way to the industrialized suburbs.

Passing by Hradčany's **Town Hall** (*Radnice*), a Renaissance structure with sgraffito, and the Hrzán Palace (*Hrzánský palác*), which is closed to the public, we continue on toward the historical **\*\*pilgrimage church of Loreto** ❹. Christoph and Kilian Ignaz Dientzenhofer designed the Baroque facade in 1720; the statues are by Josef B. Kohl and Andreas Ph. Quittainer. Every half-hour since the 17th century, a Bohemian hymn to Mary has chimed from the steeple's glockenspiel (27 bells). Notable is the **Casa Santa** (G.B. Orsi and A. Allio, 1626-31) in the inner courtyard, which was the first component of the shrine. The entire facility originated around it.

In addition to the Baroque Nativity Chapel, the focal point of this shrine, built in 1626 with funds donated by Countess Lobkowitz, is the **\*Loreto treasure**, housed on the upper floor of the cloister. Most of the sacramental gems and jewels date from the 17th and 18th centuries; the monstrance, set with over 6,000 diamonds and weighing over 12 kilograms, is of inestimable value. This gilded silver masterpiece was made in Vienna in 1699.

The uneven street of Loretánské náměstí is dominated by the **Czernin**

**Palace** ⑤ (*Černínský palác*), built by Count Czernin around 1669, and repeatedly renovated and expanded until the 1930s. Today this building, 150 meters long, houses the Foreign Ministry. The palace is the site of Prague's last defenestration: in 1948, Foreign Minister Jan Masaryk, popular son of the even more popular founder of the Republic, met his death here under circumstances which remain shrouded in mystery. The ceiling fresco over the stairway, executed in 1718 by W. L. Reiner, is called *The Fall of the Titans*. In the near-by Capuchin **Mary's Church** ⑥ (*Kostel Panny Maria Andělska*) is a lovely manger with life-size figures during the Christmas season.

A **New World** – this is how the street name ★**Nový Svět** ⑦ translates – opens a few hundred meters further on. Around 1600, famous royal astronomer Tycho Brahe lived in house No. 76 – *U zlatého noha*, To the Golden Griffon; the Baroque

*Above: In the "New World" (Nový Svět). Right: Golden Prague – the castle at night.*

building next door is the restaurant entitled The House of the Golden Pear (*U zlaté hrušky*). Also Baroque is the House of the Golden Plow (*U zlatého pluhu*) from the second half of the 17th century. Finally, there's the house called At the Golden Grape. A monument to Kepler and Tycho Brahe stands on *Parléřova ulice* at *Pohořelec*. Once a suburb of Hradčany, **Pohořelec** burned down several times, whence its name (*hořeti* means burn). But several Baroque buildings still remain, such as the *Kučerův palác*, and Broad Courtyard (*Široký dvůr*), as well as the Renaissance Golden Bough *(U zlatého stromu)*.

**St. Roch Church** ⑧ (*Kostel svatého Rocha*), at the entrance to Strahov Monastery, was built by Emperor Rudolph II after a plague epidemic in 1612. ★**Strahov Monastery** ⑨ (*Strahovský klášter*), founded in the 12th century by Premonstratensians, has undergone numerous changes in the years since. Among the most significant were those made by Giovanni Domenico Orsi (1671-79), who, with his **Theological Hall**, created one of the most magnificent rooms in Prague, a city certainly not lacking in architectural splendors. Aside from valuable folios and prints, the library contains huge globes presenting a marvelous image of science in the 17th century. The room was expanded at the end of the 18th century through the addition of the Philosophical Hall, with ceiling frescoes executed by Franz Anton Maulbertsch. The **National Museum of Texts** contains incunabula and scripts from eight centuries, ranging from early medieval manuscripts to 130,000 works of non-fiction and pamphlets and Samisdat (underground) literature from Communist Czechoslovakia.

The monastery **Church of the Assumption of the Virgin Mary** (*Kostel Panny Marie*) was built on ancient Romanesque foundations, but was renovated in the 18th century. Mozart is said to have played on the organ there.

## **LESSER TOWN / MALÁ STRANA**

Even if you have only one day to spend in Prague, don't miss the opportunity to spend a few hours on the other side of the Vtlava River in the **Lesser Town**. This romantic quarter still looks much as it did in the Baroque period; only the modern automobiles are out of sync with this image. It is well worth while to wander through alley after alley, admiring the various facades, into courtyards, and to rest a while in the cozy little squares or in the terrace-shaped parks. Even Hollywood's film-makers have come to the Vtlava: the movie *Amadeus* was not filmed on the original location of Vienna, but for a large part on Neruda Lane.

The Lesser Town first came to prominence as *Civitas nova Pragensis* after 1257, when the area below the castle was inhabited by German settlers. The first stone bridge connecting the Old Town with the Lesser Town, the now-vanished Judith Bridge, had been built a century earlier, around 1170. This bridge was washed away in a flood in 1342, to be replaced by a second stone bridge begun in 1357. The newer edifice, also linking the Lesser Town with the Old Town and New Town on the other side of the river, was built by order of Charles IV, but has only borne his name since 1870. In the year 1541, a disastrous fire destroyed a large number of the buildings in the Lesser Town; after the quarter was rebuilt, it became, in the 17th century, the district of choice for diplomats and trade missions from around the world.

### The Lesser Town Gate and Kampa Island

Most visitors access the Lesser Town via the **Charles Bridge** ❶ (*Karlův*

*Left: The Lesser Town Gate from an artist's perspective.*

*most*), which along with the castle is a world-famous symbol of the Golden City (cf page 45).

The **Lesser Town City Gate** ❷ (*Malostranská brána*) is Gothic. Some of the coats-of-arms are testimony to the regency of Wenceslas IV at the beginning of the 15th century. The gate connects the two Lesser Town Bridge Towers (*Malostranské mostecké věže*). The lower bridge tower, part of the former Judith Bridge, was built in the 12th century and is one of the oldest remaining buildings of architectural interest in Prague – despite the Renaissance cowling added in the 16th century. The higher bridge tower was built by order of George of Podiebrad in 1464 as a counterpart to the Old Town Tower. It was re-done in Gothic style by Josef Mocker between 1872-84. From the gallery there is a splendid view of the Charles Bridge, the Lesser Town, the Hradčany and the Lawrence Mountain.

**Kampa Island** ❸ is visible from the bridge. A number of mills used to operate on the banks of this narrow finger of land which is separated from the mainland by the narrow **Devil's Brook** (*Čertovka*). This latter is, in effect, Prague's Grand Canal, lined with two rows of houses to create an idyll which has inspired locals to dub this area *Benátky* (Czech for Venice). The island has always been a tranquil oasis for Prague residents. It is here that lovers meet, students and entire families sunbathe on the lawns, and tourists rest, pausing to catch their breath on one of the numerous benches under ancient shady trees. On fair days, innumerable row and pedal boats float on the Vtlava and Devil's Brook.

One of the oldest structures in the Lesser Town, first mentioned in the 12th century, is **St. John's Church of the Bleach** ❹ (*Kostel svatého Jana na prádle*) in River Lane (*Říční ulice*). Its nave dates from the 13th century; the presbytery was not added until 1641-44. A small infirmary and cemetery were also

*Lesser Town*

part of the parish. After the secularization, the church became, of all things, a public wash house, and was promptly nicknamed "House of Bleach" (*Na prádle*). In 1935, the church was completely renovated and turned over to the Czechoslovakian Hussite congregation.

The **Michna** family **palace** ❺ (*Michnův palác*) in Újezd Street, built by Francesco Caratti between 1640 and 1650, is characterized by the clear divisions of its facade. This Late Renaissance structure was used in the 19th century as, among other things, an arsenal. Diagonally opposite is the valley station of the Petřín cable railway (cf page 35).

### Around Maltese Square

Wending your way along Karmelitská, you'll arrive at **Maltese Square** ❻. When the knights of Malta arrived in Bo-

*Above: Devil's Brook separates Kampa Island from the Lesser Town. Right: The Infant Jesus of Prague in the Church of the Virgin Victorious.*

hemia in 1169, they immediately established their headquarters here on *Maltézské náměstí*. The knights of the Order of Malta had their own mill on Devil's Brook (*Čertovka*), at house No. 489. The focal point of Maltese Square is a statue of John the Baptist by Ferdinand Maximilian Brokoff.

The **House of Painters** is popular with Prague residents. Built atop a Gothic foundation, this well-preserved Renaissance structure today provides an ideal setting for a wine tavern named after the 16th-century painter Johannes Schütz who resided here. In 1660, Count Nostitz had his palace built on Maltese Square, based on plans drawn up by Francesco Caratti. The effect of the High Baroque facade is enhanced by the Rococo portal created by Anton Hafenecker (1757). Today, the Netherlands Embassy and a library are housed in the palace. Hafenecker, the father-in-law of Christoph Dientzenhofer, was one of the owners of a house in Nostitz Lane which he himself built in 1682; in 1689, it was witness to the birth of Christoph's son Kilian Ignaz, who was later to achieve equal fame.

The **palace of the Grand Maltese Prior** (*palác maltézského velkopřevora*) of this order was built by Thomas Hafenecker between 1728 and 1731. Bartolomeo Scotti later made several changes.

Today the complex and the order's monastery in Bath Lane (*Lázeňská*) 4 is once again the seat of the Maltese Order and residence of the grand prior. The palace garden walls – the **John Lennon Wall** – are adorned with a gigantic graffiti portrait of John Lennon, which is constantly getting damaged and is just as often repaired.

The **Church of St. Mary under the Chain** ❼ (*Kostel Panny Marie pod řetězem*) in neighboring Bath Lane evolved from a triple-naved Romanesque basilica. The Gothic sections were also integrated into the Baroque remodeling carried out by Carlo Lurago in the middle of the 17th century. In 1720, the architect Franciscus Maximilian Kaňka designed one of the city's loveliest gardens, the ＊**Vrtba Gardens** ❽ (*Vrtbovská zahrada*), within view of the Church of the Virgin Victorious, for the burgrave Josef Vrtba. Matthias Bernhard Braun added sculptures, vases and frescoes to this Baroque masterpiece of landscape gardening. The statues, representing heroes from ancient mythology, confer a kind of Mediterranean atmosphere upon this terraced park. From the upper terrace there is a picturesque view over the roofs of the Lesser Town to St. Nicholas' Church and to the Hradčany.

The above-mentioned Baroque ＊**Church of the Virgin Victorious** ❾ (*Kostel Panny Marie Vítězné*) was built by Prague's Lutheran congregation between 1611 and 1613. Just a decade later, in the course of re-Catholicization, it had to be returned to the Carmelites. In honor of the victory on White Mountain, the

*Lesser Town*

church was named **Maria de Victoria**. Peter Brandl created the opulent interior decorations around 1700, after the small wax statue of the **Infant Jesus of Prague** (*Pražské jezulátko*), donated to the Carmelites in 1628, had attained a kind of legendary status. The monks ascribed the power of miracles to the little statue, as it is said to have saved the city from the plague and destruction. Since then, it has been especially popular with the faithful in Spain, Italy and Latin America. The statue has over 60 robes from all over the world. Of particular beauty is the red velvet attire made by Empress Maria Theresa's very own hands.

### Market Square and Vlach Lane

The **marketplace** ❿ (*Tržiště*) was established here as early as the 14th century. It is flanked by several historically important houses, including the **House of the Golden Scale** (*U zlaté váhy*) as well as the **House of the Infant Jesus** (*U Ježíška*). This building with the pious

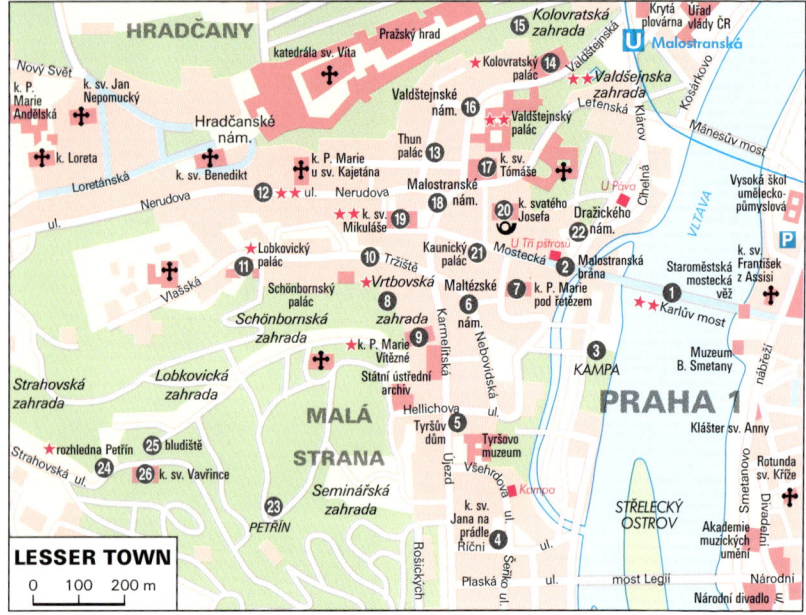

name dates from the second half of the 17th century; its Baroque façade was added later, during the years 1704-05.

Clearly the most significant building here, however, is ★**Schönborn Palace** (*Schönbornský palác*), completed in 1656, and renovated by Giovanni Santini in 1715. The palace is today home to the Embassy of the United States of America.

The ★**Lobkowicz Palace** ⑪ in Vlach Lane (*Vlašská ulice*) was built by Giovanni B. Alliprandi from 1703 to 1707. Today this magnificent structure is home to the German Embassy. In the *sala terrena* of the lovely gardens there's stucco work by Tomasso Soldati. The park contains David Černý's memorial to East Germany's refugees, who sought refuge here in 1989 – a golden Trabant on four legs. The public section of the park commands a lovely view of Hradčany; the park itself was landscaped in the first half of the 18th century.

*Right: House sign on Neruda Lane. (House of the Three Violins).*

After the turn of the 16th century, the area around Vlach Lane was inhabited by Italians. This densely-populated neighborhood, inhabited mainly by architects, artists and craftsmen, even had its own hospital (designed by Domenico Bossi in 1620), one of the first Baroque buildings in Prague, which became an orphanage after 1804.

Around 1664, Santino Bossi built a palace in *Šporkova ulice* for Count Piccolomini; later dubbed **Sporck Palace**; this was expanded in 1730, and also became an orphanage around 1850.

Fronted by a statue of the Saint from Nepomucene, the **Stonemason House** (*Kameníkův dům*) in John Lane (*Jánská ulice*) presents a picturesque aspect. In 1726, the architect and stonemason Andreas Kranner provided this lovely Renaissance building with its marvelous Rococo facade.

On a small rise of land known as John Hill (*Jánský vršek*) stand two beautiful Baroque houses from the early 17th century, facing Nerudova.

*Lesser Town*

## **Neruda Lane

The **New Castle Stairs** (*Zámécke schody*) lead up to the castle. The stairs are actually older than the Old Castle Stairs beside the Black Tower (*Černá věž*). The first documentation dates from 1278; four centuries later, the stairs were renovated and renamed the New Castle Steps.

The first houses along this romantic path were built in the 16th century. Only a few steps away is **Neruda Lane ⑫ (*Nerudova*), site of one of Prague's most renowned houses.

Originally an early Baroque structure, the legendary *House of Two Suns (*U dvou slunců*) was remodeled in 1693, whence its present appearance. The Czechs connect the house with the author Jan Neruda (1834-91) whose *Tales of the Lesser Town* is a classic piece of literature about fin-de-siècle Prague. The stories have been translated into every major language. In honor of this author, the street was renamed Nerudova ulice. The 1971

Nobel Prize winner for literature, the Chilean Pablo Neruda, took his name from the Prague author.

Giovanni Santini, architect of numerous Bohemian structures, created one of his most beautiful works in 1720-25 when he built the **Thun-Hohenstein Palace** for Count Kolowrat, one of two Thun palaces in Prague. This palace later fell to the hands of another family. Although this building, which today houses the Italian Embassy, is not open to the public, the statues by Matthias B. Braun above the portal give some impression of the grandeur of 18th-century Prague.

Across the street, the **Morzin Palace**, constructed for Countess Morzin in the short span of just two years (1713-14), is another proof of Santini's talents. Today housing the Romanian Embassy, the building is ornamented with larger-than-life figures of Moors, featured on the Morzin coat-of-arms and created in the workshop of Ferdinand Maximilian Brokoff. This famous sculptor also crafted the Baroque busts *Day and Night*

*Information pages 60-63*

as well as the depiction of the four regions of the earth that were recognized at that time. Santini lived for two decades in the neighboring Valkoun Renaissance house *(Valkounsky dům;* No. 14), which was remodeled by Christoph Dientzenhofer in 1704 in Baroque style.

The *★House of the Three Violins* (*U tří housliček*) next door is a favorite subject for photographers; for over a century it belonged to a family of violin-makers. On the other side of the Dientzenhofer house is the **House of the Golden Goblet** (*U zlaté číše*), named in memory of a family of goldsmiths. Near the **House of the Golden Carp** (*U zlatého kapr)* in the Thunovská, with its lovely 16th-century Renaissance gable, are the quarters of the British Embassy in a Baroque building by Carlo Lugaro. The Salzburg Archbishop, Guidobald Thun-Hohenstein, had this palace expanded in the years after 1659; it has become known as the **Thun Pal-**

*Above: In the Waldstein Gardens. Right: Night in the Lesser Town.*

ace ⑬ (*Thun palác*). Nearby are other palaces: Ignazio Palliardi created the Baroque facade of the **Ledebour Palace** (*Ledeburský palác*); on the other side of the Valdštejnské náměstí is the **Auersperg Palace** (*Auersperský palác*). The magnificent **Fürstenberg Palace** (*Fürstenbergský palác*) in Waldstein Lane (*Valdštejnská*) 8 is today the seat of the Polish Embassy.

One of the loveliest palaces in the Lesser Town was created by Ignazio Palliardi in the 1780s for Count Czernin, the *★Kolowrat Palace* ⑭ (*Kolvratský palác*). The palace was later owned by the Kolowrat family. The atmosphere is simply infatuating: across the way is a wing of the Waldstein Palace, and nearby is the **palace of the magnates of the Pálffy family** (*Pálffyovský palác*), who once had extensive land holdings in upper Hungary. The **Kolowrat Gardens** ⑮ in Waldstein Lane (*Valdštejnská*) are considered to be one of the last Baroque parks in Prague; this fanciful facility even includes a small observation tower.

*Lesser Town*

## **Waldstein Palace and **Waldstein Gardens

**Waldstein Square** ⑯ (*Valdštejnské náměstí*) is the site of one of the city's main attractions. Albrecht von Waldstein (Wallenstein) commissioned the architects Andrea Spezza, Giovanni Pierroni and Nicola Sebregondi to build him a mighty palace within sight of the castle. The construction of **Waldstein Palace** (*Valdštejnský palác;* 1623-30) represented a turning point in the development of the Lesser Town. The middle portal on the front is a part of the former Trčka Palace, the original Renaissance residence which served as the core of this monumental palace. In his delusions of grandeur, Waldstein had scenes from the Trojan War painted in the *sala terrena*. But Waldstein was not able to enjoy his palace for long. Only four years following its completion, the greedy military commander, who had for years enriched himself at the cost of others, was murdered in Eger (Cheb). As the palace was being built, the splendid **Waldstein Gardens** (*Valdštejnská zahrada*) were also laid out. Records show that a total of two dozen houses, three large gardens and a brick works had to be razed to make way for the palace and its grounds. The original sculptures, created by Adrian de Vries of Holland, were carried off by the Swedes as part of the spoils of the Thirty Years' War. Today they decorate the park of the Drottningholm Royal Castle near Stockholm, and what you see here in Prague are merely well-made copies. (Until 2001, the Waldstein Gardens are only accessible via the Letenská on account of renovations).

### Around the Lesser Town Ring

Passing through *Letenská ulice*, you approach the Lesser Town Ring (*Malostranské náměstí*). **St. Thomas Church** ⑰ (*Kostel svatého Tomáše*) was a part of the convent of the Augustinians who settled in Bohemia at the end of the 13th century. Their place of worship was

*Above: The massive edifice of St. Nicholas Church in the Lesser Town.*

renovated in Renaissance style in the late 16th century; between 1723 and 1731, Kilian Ignaz Dientzenhofer bestowed on it the Baroque style seen today. In 1639, two paintings by Peter Paul Rubens – *The Torture of St. Thomas* and *Portrait of St. Augustine* – adorned the main altar; today, these are displayed in the National Gallery in the Sternberg Palace. The interior of the church is also opulent Baroque. The frescoes of Augustine by Wenzel Lorenz Reiner include *The Baptism* and *The Apotheosis of the Saints.* Anyone who feels in need of a rest at this point might want to try the dark strong beer served in the monastery's tavern.

Only a streetcar track separates St. Thomas Church from one of the **Lobkowitz Palaces**. This Renaissance structure, later redone in Baroque style, had a number of aristocratic owners before it was turned into a school. The original floor plan of the late Renaissance

**Town Hall** (*Radnice*) on the east side of the **Lesser Town Ring** ⓲ (*Malostranské náměstí*), built from 1617 to 1622 by Giovanni Bossi, is, despite later renovations, still evident. The stairwell has Rococo sculptures by Ignaz Platzer dating from the second half of the 18th century. Opposite is the **Liechtenstein Palace** (*Liechtenštejnský palác*). Karel von Liechtenstein, one of the leaders of the Counter-Reformation, bought five Burgher houses here, which he had transformed into a palace in 1638. Its classical facade was added in 1791. Today it houses the Music Academy.

The **Sternberg Palace** (*Šternberský palác*), built at the end of the 17th century, dominates the north side of the Lesser Town Ring with its lovely Baroque facade. In 1541, the neighboring house, *On the Bastion*, was the starting-place of a catastrophic fire which not only destroyed large sections of the Lesser Town within a matter of hours, but also took its toll on Hradčany and even the castle. The late Renaissance **palace** of the

**Smiřický** family (*Smiřický palác*), served in the 17th century as headquarters for the Bohemian aristocracy's rebellion against the Hapsburgs. It was here on May 22, 1618 that the rebellion against the Hapsburgs was planned, and which led the following day to the tossing of the Hapsburg civil servants from a window.

The Lesser Town is dominated by one of Europe's loveliest buildings, on which a number of first-rate Baroque artists demonstrated their talents: the imposing **\*\*St. Nicholas Church** ⑲ (*Kostel svatého Mikuláše*), built for the powerful Jesuit order. This church, with its Italian influence, was completed in three phases. Christoph Dientzenhofer began construction in 1704-11. His son, Kilian Ignaz, added the presbytery and the dome (1737-52); his son-in-law, Anselmo Lurago, built the steeple in 1755-56. Particularly noteworthy, a true gem of Baroque art, is the 1,500-square-meter ceiling fresco, one of the largest on the Continent. Johann Lukas Kracker worked on this painting, depicting the life of St. Nicholas, for almost ten years. Franz Xaver Palko painted most of the altarpieces, while the *Pietá*, the fresco in the cupola and the decoration of the lofts are by Karel Škréta. Ignaz Platzer the Elder as well as Richard and Peter Prachner crafted the statues and pulpit.

The Jesuit College next to St. Nicholas Church was built between 1676 and 1690 by the Italian Domenico Orsi. It was disbanded in 1773. The **Column of the Holy Trinity** before the church is the work of Italian Giovanni Alliprandi (1714).

One of the well-preserved Renaissance houses along the Lesser Town Ring is the **House of the Golden Lion** (*U zlatého lva*). The popular wine restaurant, **House of the Patron** (*U mecenáše*), is housed under the ground floor's vaulted ceiling. Dating from 1608, this house is also known as "Trost House" for its erstwhile owner Wenzel Trost of Tiefenthal. The classical house next door was originally

Baroque, built by Christoph Dientzenhofer.

**St. Joseph's Church** ⑳ (*Kostel svatého Josefa*); consecrated in 1692) was the first House of God of the Carmelite Monastery. Matthäus Wenzel Jäckel and Peter Brandl embellished its interior. Anton Schmidt built the Rococo urban **Kaunitz Palace** ㉑ for Count Kaunitz in Bridge Lane (*Mostecká ulice*) between 1773 and 1775. The statues are the work of Ignaz Platzer. On **Dražického náměstí** ㉒, at the Charles University School of Medicine, there's a statue of Saints Cosmas and Damian (1709). Johann Fux, royal supplier of plumes, had the unusual **House of the Three Ostriches** (*Dům u tří pštrosů*) built just below Charles Bridge in 1585. It was here that the second coffee house in Prague was opened in 1714. Now renovated, it houses a first-class hotel and restaurant.

### Lawrence Mountain

A hike up **Lawrence Mountain** ㉓ (*Petřín*) is highly recommended, but there is a cable railway to the top as well. From the 60-meter-high Observation Deck of the miniature **\*Eiffel Tower** ㉔, there is a splendid view. This "little brother" of the Paris original was erected on the occasion of the 1891 Industrial Fair and served until the end of the 1980's as a telecommunications tower. There are 299 steps up to the observation gallery. In the adjacent **Mirror Labyrinth** ㉕ you can laugh at your grossly distorted reflection.

The original Romanesque **St. Lawrence Church** ㉖ (*Kostel svatého Vavřince*) developed into a Baroque edifice. The church's patron saint later lent his name to the entire hill. The **Wall of Hunger** was part of the Medieval city's fortifications. The pleasure palace **Villa Kinských**, built in the Empire style, and the extensive parks make Lawrence Mountain a popular excursion destination for Prague's inhabitants and their guests.

*Lesser Town*

## **OLD TOWN / STARÉ MĚSTO

### From the **Powder Tower to the **Old Town Ring

For centuries, the **Powder Tower** ❶ (*Prašná brána*), has guarded the access to the Royal Mile. The Bohemian King Johann of Luxembourg and his wife Eliška trod this path up to the Hradčany for the first time in the 14th century. They were followed by Emperor Charles IV at the start of his reign. The Powder Tower, also a city gate, was built around 1478 according to plans by Matthias Reiseck and was given a Gothic style in 1875-86 by Josef Mocker.

Do take the time to visit the lovely **Municipal (Representative) Building** ❷ (*Obecní dům*) opposite the Powder Tower on Republic Square (*nám. Republiky*). The art nouveau building was erected in 1905-1911 on the spot of the former Royal Court. Art nouveau star Alfons Mucha participated in the colorful appointments, along with Myslbek, Aleš, Šaloun, Švabinský and others. The restaurants and the cafe are often used by tour groups; the monumental Smetana Hall is an impressive concert hall. Past the Powder Tower, and continuing through the lively pedestrian zone of *Celetná ❸ to the Old Town Ring, with its lovely historic residences and former palaces, you'll pass the **House of the Three Kings** (*U tři králů*), where Franz Kafka lived from 1896 to 1907, and the Cubist house *U Černé Matky boží*, built in 1912 by Josef Gočár, and decorated with a Baroque statue of the Black Madonna. A small Cubism museum is located here.

The **Old Town Ring** ❹ (*Staroměstké nám.*), the lively heart of the Old Town, is always animated with street artists, hawkers and visitors from all over the world. The gigantic statue of the reformer Jan Hus (Ladislav Šaloun, 1915),

*Left: The Old Town Ring and Tyn Church.*

and the many historical buildings around the square form a delightful backdrop for the lively hustle and bustle. Easter and Christmas markets are held here.

**Tyn Church** ❺ (*Kostel Panny Marie před Týnem*), its steeple measuring over 80 meters and its Madonna visible from afar, is one of Prague's most impressive churches. Parts of this structure, where Danish astronomer Tycho Brahe was laid to rest in 1601, were built by craftsmen from the Parler workshop at the end of the 14th century. The interior is partially Gothic; Baroque elements were added later. Karel Škréta, born near here, painted the altarpieces (before 1660). This triple-naved church with its three presbyteries served as Protestant headquarters until the Thirty Years' War.

Behind Tyn Church, the Malá Štupartská leads to the triple naved Gothic **St. Jacob's Church** ❻ (*Kostel svatého Jakuba*) with its Minorite monastery. In the late 17th and early 18th centuries, this 14th-century church, a popular venue for concerts, was given a new Baroque face by J.S. Pánke. Peter Brandl and W.L. Reiner painted most of the pictures for its 21 altars. The frescoes in this church, Prague's second-largest, are by F.Q. Voget, who also decorated the rooms of the cloister.

Until well into the 16th century, newly-arrived merchants lodged – for a fee – in the narrow alleys around **Tyn Court** (also called Ungelt) under the patronage of the reigning king. The royal court had a vested interest in trade (and the resulting customs duties) until 1774. The Renaissance loggia in the **Granovský Palace** is from 1560.

The National Gallery exhibits its collection of graphic works in the city's most beautiful Rococo palace, the **Goltz-Kinský Palace** ❼ (*palác Goltz-Kinských*), built in 1755-65 by Anselmo Lurago, based on plans by Kilian Ignaz Dientzenhofer and decorated with sculptures by Ignaz Platzer. Countess Kinsky

(1843-1914) was born here. Under her married name, Bertha von Suttner, she became famous for her work *Lay Down Your Arms!* which protested the insanity of the arms build-up. This pacifist and author was awarded the Nobel Peace Prize in 1905.

Until the mid-19th century, the Renaissance **House of the Stone Bells** (*U kamenného zvonu*), beside the Goltz-Kinsky Palace, housed the **Tyn School** (*Týnská škola*). Romanesque and Gothic traits bear testimony to its earlier use. Today, the **Prague City Gallery** is located here. In the adjacent early classic **House of the White Unicorn** (*U bílého jednorožce*), excavations have revealed a Romanesque room. Above it, a Gothic arcade with well-preserved cross-rib vaulting stretches the length of the room.

The **\*\*Old Town's Town Hall** ⑧ (*Staroměstké radnice*) is composed of several buildings, which ever since the

*Above: The Old Town Town Hall. Right: The famous clock on the Old Town Town Hall.*

14th century have gradually come to be public buildings. A wedding ceremony held in the town hall is considered an important social event. Every schoolchild in Bohemia knows Václav Brožík's painting entitled *Jan Hus in Front of the Council of Constance*, which hangs in the assembly room here. Brožík also painted the monumental *The Election of George von Poděbrady as King of Bohemia*. There is a magnificent view from the 70-meter-high Town Hall Tower. The **\*\*Town Hall Astronomical Clock** looks much the same as it has for the past 500 years. Dating originally from 1410, it was reconstructed in 1490 and mechanized in 1560. On the hour, two windows open in the tower above: Christ and the Twelve Apostles pass by. Death rings the knell, reminding us that our time here on earth is limited. He nods at the miserly, the vain and the Turks. But they nod back, for they are not yet ready to die. A crowing cock ends the little drama, the full hour has struck. The clock also provides the current phase of the moon and the position of the planets. The lower part has a copy of the calendar with zodiac signs painted by Josef Mánes in 1865. The original is located in the Museum of the Capital City of Prague. One building in the complex stands out: the Renaissance **House of the Minute** (*U minuty*), covered with sgraffiti.

On the south side of the square is the **House of the Golden Unicorn** (*U zlatého jednorožce*) in which Bedřich Smetana established a music school in 1848. Restored frescoes by Mikoláš Aleš adorn the publishing house **Štorchův dům**, while the **House of the Golden Angel** (*U zlatého anděla*) sports a Baroque statue of St. Florian by Ignaz Platzer.

The east side of the Old Town Ring is dominated by **St. Nicholas Church** ❾ (*Kostel svatého Mikuláše*). This masterpiece by Kilian Ignaz Dientzenhofer was built in the amazingly short span of four years (1732-35). The octagonal cupola of the opulent church – now belonging to the Hussite congregation – was frescoed by Cosmas Damian Asam. In U radnice 5, next to St. Nicholas Church, the German-Jewish writer **Franz Kafka** was born on July 3, 1883. A bronze plaque on the wall of the house and a permanent exhibit draw many literary enthusiasts.

Old Town

### Gallus Quarter

German immigrants founded the **Gallus Quarter** in the 13th century. This neighborhood encompassed the Coal Market and Fruit Market as well as Knight Street (*Rytířská*) and Galli Lane (*Havelská*). From the Powder Tower, continue along the Celetná, but turn left after a few paces to the **Fruit Market** ❿ (*Ovocný trh*). A daily fruit, vegetable and flower market is held here; glass items, pottery and other souvenirs are also sold.

The **\*Carolinum** ⓫, one of the oldest extant universities in central Europe, was founded in 1348 by Charles IV. The

lovely Gothic oriel, all that's left of the university chapel dedicated to St. Cosmas and St. Damian, is an architectural feature of note. The Carolinum was able to withstand the pressure from the Jesuit college in the Clementinum, which was founded to serve as a counterweight to this secular educational institution during the Counter-Reformation. Receiving a diploma in the auditorium of Charles University has always been considered one of the greatest honors.

Between 1781 and 1783, a century before the National Theater was built, Anton Hafenecker built the **Estates Theater** ⓬ (*Stavovské divadlo*) here. In 1834, the theater presented the singspiel *Fidlovačka* by František Škroup, with a libretto by Josef Kajetán Tyl. Tyl's poem *Kde domov můj* (*Where is my home, my native land?*) became the text of the national anthem. In 1949 the theater, now a part of the National Theater, was renamed the Tyl Theater (*Tylovo divadlo*) in his honor. An even more important world premiere given here was that of Mozart's

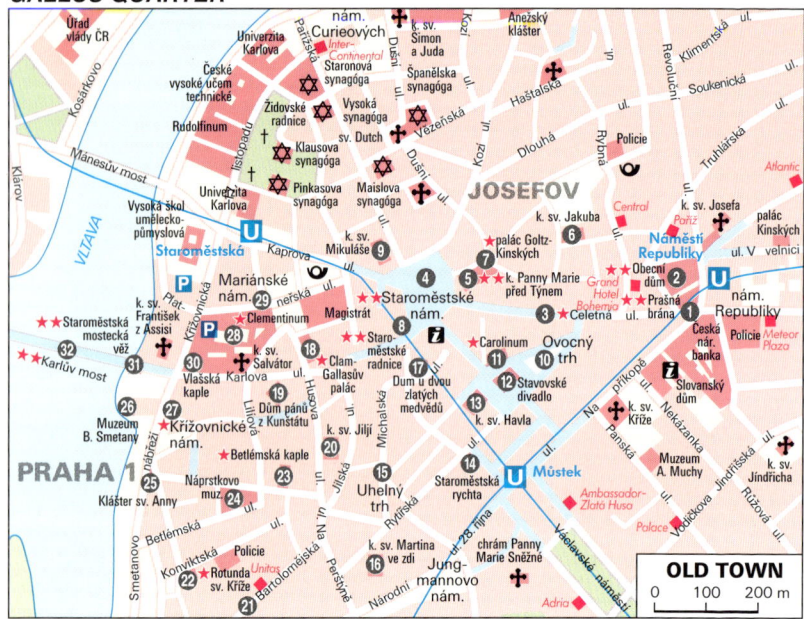

OLD TOWN
0    100    200 m

*Don Giovanni* in 1787. The former Early Baroque **Kolowrat Palace** (*Kolovratský palác;* Domenico Orsi, 1697), its original appointments preserved, is part of the Estates Theater.

**St. Gallus Church** ⑬ (*Kostel svatého Havla*), originally a Romanesque structure, was Gothicized in the first half of the 14th century, and later adorned with Baroque elements. Noteworthy are the lancet arch portal and the cross-rib vaulting. The tomb of prolific Baroque painter Karel Škréta is located here. The arcades of Havelská, often used as backdrop for historical films, convey a sense of the city's past appearance, an impression supported by buildings such as the House of the Golden Scale, Roland House, or the House of the Bohemian Crown.

A conglomerate of several styles (Gothic, Renaissance, Baroque) can be seen in the **House of the Old Town Magistrate** ⑭ (*Staroměstská rychta*) on

*Right: Fruit Market with St. Gallus Church in the background.*

Knight Street. The same is true of **Hrobčický Palace** and **House of the Blue Column** (*U modrého sloupu*) and **House of the Golden Wheel** (*U zlatého kola*). The Socialists used two splendid palaces here for propaganda purposes. The neo-Renaissance building of the Prague Savings Bank served as a Klement Gottwald Museum, while the former Baroque Monastery of the Mendicant Carmelites sheltered the "House of Soviet Science and Culture" for decades.

From here, it's only a matter of steps to the historic **Coal Market** ⑮ (*Uhelný trh*), at the center of which is the splendid Empire-style Wimmer fountain from 1797, representing an allegory in praise of viticulture and agriculture. Charcoal was sold here from the Middle Ages until the early 19th century. A memorial plaque on **Platýz House** notes that Franz Liszt once stayed there. The **House of the Three Golden Lions** (*U tří zlatých lvů*), with a wine tavern, belonged at the end of the 18th century to the Dušeks, a musical couple who once hosted W.A. Mozart. A

Old Town

relief and a memorial plaque commemorate the composer's visit in 1787.

From here we make a brief detour to Martinská, where one of the oldest churches in Prague is located: **Church of St. Martin in the Wall** ⓰ (*Kostel svatého Martina ve zdi*). This used to mark the boundary between the Old and New Towns. Originally dating from the late 12th century, this Romanesque church was renovated in Gothic style after 1350 and again around 1490. Both the Gothic and the Romanesque elements are still visible, particularly the lovely Gothic web vaulting. It is administered by the Congregation of Bohemian Brothers. It was here, in 1414, that communion was offered for the first time to everyone, not only to priests. The chalice has been a revolutionary symbol for the Hussites ever since.

Wandering through Melantrichova, the visitor stumbles upon a couple of historic, originally Gothic residences and businesses with names such as **The Red Heart** (*U červeného srdce*), and the former Romanesque-Gothic **St. Michael's Church** with its monastery (*Byvaly klášteř servitu u svatého Michala*). Literature fans will want to visit the house on **Leather Lane** (*Kožná*) where the reporter Egon Erwin Kisch (1885-1948) was born: the **House of the Two Golden Bears** ⓱ (*U dvou zlatých medvědů*) boasts a marvelous Renaissance portal.

### From the **Old Town Ring to **Charles Bridge

Close to the bustling Old Town Ring, the **Lesser Town Ring** (*Malé nám.*), only a few feet away from the Town Hall, is nevertheless a tranquil oasis. At the intersection of Charles / Hus Lanes (*Karlova / Husova*), turn to the right to the magnificent ★**Clam-Gallas Palace** ⓲ (*Clam-Gallasův palác*). It was built between 1713-19 by Johann B. Fischer of Erlach for Marshall Count Gallas, who served as viceroy of Naples. He commissioned only first-class Baroque artists. Matthias B. Braun sculpted the giants beside the portal as well as the Triton fountain statue in the First Courtyard and the figures on the stairway (stucco work by G. Fiumberti, R. Boll); Carlo Carlone produced the frescoes in the stairway and in the reception rooms. Shortly after its completion, the palace passed into the hands of Count Clam. Today it houses the **Prague city archives**, with hundreds of thousands of documents and valuable Prague ephemera. Concerts are often held here. Back to the Karlova / Husova intersection, follow Husova to the South. A detour to the right leads towards the Vtlava River on Chain Lane (*Řetězová*). The **Čapek Mansion** ⓳ (*U Čapků* or *Dům pánů z Kunštátu*) was built in 1200 and is one of the most significant Romanesque secular buildings that's yet been excavated in Prague. A number of rooms provide a good impression of life in the Middle Ages. Back on Husova, you'll find, besides a couple of old residential houses, one of the loveliest churches in Prague: **St. Giles' Church** ⓴ (*Kostel svatého Jiljí*). This Romanesque edifice was taken over from the Hussites in 1625 by the Dominicans who turned it into a Baroque jewel. The carved confessional from 1720 and the altarpiece and the ceiling frescoes by Wenzel Lorenz Reiner are particularly impressive. Reiner (1689-1743) lived nearby, in the House of the Dukes (*U Herzogů*), the so-called **Pernstein House** at 5 Na Perštýně and is buried here in the church. Next door is the popular restaurant **House of the Small Bears** (*U medvídků*).

**Bartolomějská ulice** ㉑ (Bartholomew Street) boasts two noteworthy sights: the **Jesuit commune** (consecrated in 1660) with its concert hall and the High Baroque **St. Bartholomew's Church**. The latter was built between 1726 and 1731 according to plans drawn up by K.I. Dientzenhofer, and decorated with fres-

*Right: Jan Hus the teacher. Fresco in the Betlehem Chapel.*

coes by W.L. Reiner. One of the oldest examples of Romanesque art in the Old Town is on Světlá Street, where the popular storyteller and novelist Karolina Světlá (1830-99) was born. The early-12th-century **★Holy Cross Rotunda** ㉒ (*Rotunda svatého Kříže*) was saved from the wrecker's ball in the 1860s, and has since been restored. The frescoes which remain, however, are Gothic.

Two tiny streets, *Konviktská* and *Betlémská,* lead to *Betlémské náměstí*. The **★Bethlehem Chapel** ㉓ (*Betlémská kaple*), a national landmark, is considered an authentic replica of the original late 14th-century church in which Jan Hus preached between 1402 and 1413. In 1786 the chapel was torn down, leaving only the surrounding walls standing. A residential house was later built on the site, and in the early 1950s archaeologists discovered fragments of earlier inscriptions. The reformer Jan Hus was held in high esteem even during the times of the "atheist" Communist regime. Before his exile, he was the Rector of Charles University. When he refused to swear allegiance to the Pope, his summons to appear before the Council was inevitable. Despite his promise of safe conduct, Emperor Sigismund ordered Hus burned at the stake in Constance on July 6, 1415. This date is now a public holiday.

The magnificent **Náprstkovo Museum** ㉔ is located in the house *U Halánků*. It contains a respectable collection of ethnography, started in the last century by the Vojtěc Náprstek, and includes works from Oceania, Africa and Asia as well as pre-Columbian America.

Strolling on through the characteristic narrow alleys of the Old Town, you'll come to *Anenské náměstí* and the **Dominican St. Anne's Convent** ㉕ (*Klášter svatého Anny*). This 14th-century building with its original Gothic roof timbering, renovated in Baroque style in the 17th century, houses the remains of the Romanesque Lawrence Rotunda, discov-

*Old Town*

ered in the 1950s. Christoph Willibald Gluck played here. Both Mozart and Beethoven resided in the **Pachta Palace** (*Pachtovský palác*) next door during their stays in Prague. Across the street in the **House of the Green Hat** (*U zeleného kloboučku*) is the **Theater on the Balustrade** (*Divadlo na zábradlí*), formerly one of Europe's leading theaters by virtue of its trailblazing productions. The intimate house was also made famous by the pantomime ensemble of Ladislav Fialka.

Just a few steps further is the Old Town Water Tower dating from the end of the 15th century. The former city waterworks, with its impressive sgraffito decorations, was converted in 1936 into one of Prague's most popular **museums** ㉖, devoted to the composer **Bedřich Smetana**. Between the two buildings is a little oasis, a cafe on the banks of the Vltava.

Focal point of ★**Crusaders' Square** ㉗ (*Křížovnické náměstí*) is another statue of Charles IV, unveiled in 1848 in honor of the 500th anniversary of the founding of Prague's *Carolinum* University.

Two religious structures enhance the architectural beauty of the square. The first of these, **St. Francis Church** (*Kostel svatého Františka Serafinského*) with its adjacent **Monastery of the Crusaders with the Red Star** (designed by Carlo Lurago), the only order founded in Bohemia during the crusades, has stood here since the middle of the 13th century. In the crypt of this church, designed by Jean B. Mathey and built by Domenico Canevale in the 1680s, the remains of an early Gothic Church of the Holy Ghost can still be seen. In addition to the building's sculptures, both inside and out, and the paintings around the altar, a noteworthy art work here is the fresco of *The Last Judgment* by W.L. Reiner (1722). The second, **St. Salvator Church** (*Kostel svatého Salvatora*), originally built in Renaissance style and later renovated in Baroque, is part of the Clementinum. The figures on the front facade are by Johann Georg Bendl.

Once a center for the Jesuit order, the ★**Clementinum** ㉘, Prague's largest com-

plex of related buildings, apart from the castle, presently holds the church of the Greek Orthodox congregation. **St. Clemens Church** (*Kostel svatého Klimenta*), was built by Kilian Ignaz Dientzenhofer between 1711 and 1713, and elaborately appointed by a number of artists: the sculptures are by Matthias B. Braun, the altarpiece by Peter Brandl, and the ceiling frescoes by Johann Hiebl.

After 1653, the Jesuit College expanded steadily on its 2-hectare site, creating a veritable fortress of spirituality (larger parts, such as the chapel of mirrors or the astronomers' tower, are the work of Franciscus M. Kaňka). The Clementinum is considered a gem of the Baroque and Rococo. Especially notable are the **reading room** (formerly the refectory) and **library**, with their decorative stucco work and frescoes. The **Great Hall** (1722) houses old clocks and outsized globes

*Above: Musicians on the Charles Bridge. Right: View from the Old Town Bridge Tower to the stream of tourists on the Charles Bridge.*

from the 17th and 18th century. Daily weather readings have been taken in the Clementinum since the 18th century; this post is the longest meteorological observation in the world.

At **Square of Our Lady Mary** ㉙ (*Mariánské náměstí*), is one of the formerly "richest" fountains in the world: the allegorical depiction of the Vtlava so pleased a captain of the horse that he left his entire fortune to it. One of the beneficiaries later sued the sculpture "Theresia" and won the dispute.

Resident Italian craftsmen built the **Vlach Chapel** ㉚ (*Vlašská kaple*) around 1590 in Charles Lane (*Karlova ulice*). Charles Lane is adorned with numerous palaces (Colloredo-Mansfeld, Pötting) and venerable edifices such as **The Golden Fountain** (*U zlaté studně;* No. 3), and **The Blue Pike** (*U modré štiky*; No. 20). **The Golden Snake** (*U zlatého hada*; house No. 18) on Liliová ulice is popular, for Prague's first coffee house was opened here in 1714 by an Armenian. A restaurant is now located here.

## **Old Town Bridge Tower and **Charles Bridge

The **Old Town Bridge Tower  (*Staroměstská mostecká věž*) is a masterpiece by Peter Parler: the east facade and the webbed vaulting in the tower's archway are also the work of this German architect. On the right side of the portal is a portrait of the eponymous Charles IV, king and emperor; the figure on the left is his son Wenceslas IV. From the observation gallery there is a fantastic view over the bridge, the river and Hradčany.

**Charles Bridge 32 (*Karlův most*) has borne this name since 1870 when it was renamed in honor of Emperor Charles IV. The regent, well aware of the strategic significance of Prague's location at the crossroads of important trade routes, ordered this stone bridge built in 1357 after an earlier bridge on the site had been washed away. He was very interested in astrology, and therefore chose the date for the corner stone based on a magical pyramid of uneven numbers: 1 3 5 7 9 7 5 3 1. Construction began in the year 1357, on 9.7. at 5:31 in the morning. "His" architect, the German Peter Parler, who was also working on St. Vitus Cathedral, drew up a plan for a bridge with 16 arches stretching some 516 meters across the river, and almost 10 meters wide. This site, where today crowds of tourists jostle and photograph, once served as a marketplace and jousting field. Prague Bridge, as it used to be more simply known, was even said to be used for executions.

The **statue of the Nepomucene**, cast in Nuremberg (based on a design by M. Rauchmüller and Johann Brokoff's subsequent model) in 1683, is the oldest statue on the bridge. From this spot, the former confessor of the Bohemian queen was thrown into the Vtlava in a sack, for he refused to divulge to King Wenceslas his wife's confessional secrets. His sainthood was officially proclaimed at the beginning of the 17th century. Since then he has been considered the Bohemian patron saint, as well as the patron saint of bridges. His stone image can be seen on many bridges in the country. During the Baroque period, Bohemia's leading sculptors were asked to create statues for the sandstone bridge; the best-known are Johann Brokoff and his sons Ferdinand Maximilian and Johann Josef Michael, as well as Matthias B. Braun, Johann Friedrich Kohl and Matthäus W. Jäckel. Most of their original statues, badly damaged by smog and acid rain, have been replaced by copies. More statues, many of them by J. and E. Max, were added around 1850, including that of the national patron saint Václav (St. Wenceslas). The most recent sculpture group, depicting the saints Cyril and Methodius, was created by K. Dvořák between 1928 and 1938. Particularly impressive are the depiction of the Ottomans guarding the captured Christians (F.M. Brokoff, 1714), the vision of St. Luitgard (Braun, 1710), and the crucifix by Hans Hillger (1629).

*Old Town*

## **JOSEFOV /
THE JEWISH QUARTER

Two figures are practically synony-mous with Prague's Jewish quarter. One is a real-life figure whose life's work was long treated as a phantom; the other is a phantom whom people claim to have seen haunting the gas-lit alleys and passage-ways of the Old Town. The characters in question are Franz Kafka and the Golem.

Kafka (1883-1924, buried in the family plot in the Jewish Cemetery in Olšany) was born in the Josefov (corner of Maislova and Kaprova), and later lived on the *Pařížská*. He was a literary *persona non grata* in Communist Czechoslovakia until 1963, when Prague German scholar Professor Eduard Goldstuecker restored Kafka to grace at a literary conference in Liblice with the air of a magician pulling a rabbit out of a hat.

Much more popular at the time was the mystical figure of the homunculus Go-lem, created in the waning years of the Middle Ages and first introduced into lit-erature in the 18th century. English-lan-guage readers may be familiar with him through the stories of Isaac Bashevis Singer; the figure's original creator was Jehuda ben Bezalel, also known as Rabbi Loew. The rabbi's memorial, in the form of a statue by prominent sculptor Ladislav Šaloun, stands on Square of Our Lady Mary (*Mariánské náměstí*), in front of the Old Town's new Town Hall.

Between these two poles – the myth of the ghetto and the reality of Jewish life and suffering in the 20th century, includ-ing the Holocaust of tens of thousands at the hands of the Nazis – lies the history of the Old Town district known as Josefov, or the Jewish quarter. The Holocaust all but destroyed it. Today, the Jewish com-munity has only 1,000 members; there were 40,000 before the Second World War. The Old Town's Jewish quarter,

*Left: Art nouveau detail.*

densely populated since the 12th century, was dubbed "Joseph's Town" in 1850 in honor of Emperor Joseph II, who became king of Bohemia in 1780. Maria Theresa's son instituted reforms which helped to ease living conditions for the Jewish population. Jews were no longer forced to wear the yellow mark; they could work without restrictions as crafts-men; they could attend public schools and the university. In 1788, Prague University awarded degrees in medicine to the first two Jewish doctors. And yet, Jews were repeatedly reminded of the fact that they were only a tolerated minority, albeit rel-atively strong in number. What this meant in practice was the publication of lam-poons and anti-Semitic pamphlets, which were then circulated between Prague and Vienna, denouncing the "uselessness and perniciousness of the Jews in the king-dom." In 1783, 8,532 Jews (and nine Christians) were registered in the ghetto. A hundred years later, only one-third of the inhabitants were Jewish.

Six synagogues, the Old Jewish Ceme-tery and the Town Hall are the only re-maining structures of the historic ghetto. The rest were destroyed at the turn of this century, the victims of "*Assanierung*," the Austrian term for "improving buildings for reasons of hygiene, society, or other considerations." Where today there are ten streets, there were 31 alleyways in the 1890s; where 80 buildings now stand, there were once 290. The population den-sity in the Jewish district was the highest in Prague, with more than 1,820 inhabit-ants per hectare. The death rate was 50% higher than in the other city districts.

The "improvements" created the main thoroughfare of **Parisian Boulevard** (*Pařížská třída*), 24 meters wide. The ele-gant boulevard leads from the Old Town Ring to the banks of the Vtlava. With its art nouveau facades and its eclecticism, Paris Street is now a highly sought ad-dress for offices and businesses of re-puted international companies.

*Josefov*

## *Rudolfinum

For those discovering Prague by metro, get off at the Staromestka station. Before viewing the Jewish quarter, it is worth glancing at the *Rudolfinum ❶ on nám. Jana Palacha.

The spiritual fathers of the National Theater, Josef Zitek and Josef Schulz also provided the designs for the neo-Renaissance Rudolfinum. It was constructed from 1876 to 1884 on the west bank of the Vtlava close to the Old Jewish Cemetery. The Attica is adorned with statues of Czechoslovakian artists and composers.

The building was named in honor of the Czechoslovakian Crown Prince Rudolph. In the First Czech Republic and shortly after the Second World War, the National Assembly sat here.

Since 1946, the Rudolfinum has been the seat of the Czechoslovakian Philharmonic. Concerts are held in the Dvořák Hall during the "Prague Spring."

*Above: In the Old Jewish Cemetery.*

## *Pinkas Synagogue and the **Old Jewish Cemetery

From the Rudolfinum, the *Pinkas Synagogue ❷ (*Pinkasova synagóga*) and thus the entrance to the Old Jewish Cemetery (*Starý židovské hřbitov*) in Broad Lane are quickly reached. Both of these, along with the Maisl, Cell and Spanish Synagogues and the Hall of Ceremonies are part of the **Jewish Museum.

After the Second World War, the synagogue was made into an impressive memorial to the Jewish victims of the Nazis. Carved into the synagogue's wall in alphabetical order are the data pertaining to the Jews from the Reich's protectorate of Bohemia and Moravia who fell victim to the racial delusions of Hitler's Germany. 77,297 names, birth dates, deportation dates and dates of death form the world's largest grave inscription. Rabbi Pinkas founded the synagogue in 1479. The prayer-room harbors subterranean rooms, including a ritual bath (*mikwe*) and a spring. Archaeologists date these back to

*Information pages 60-63*

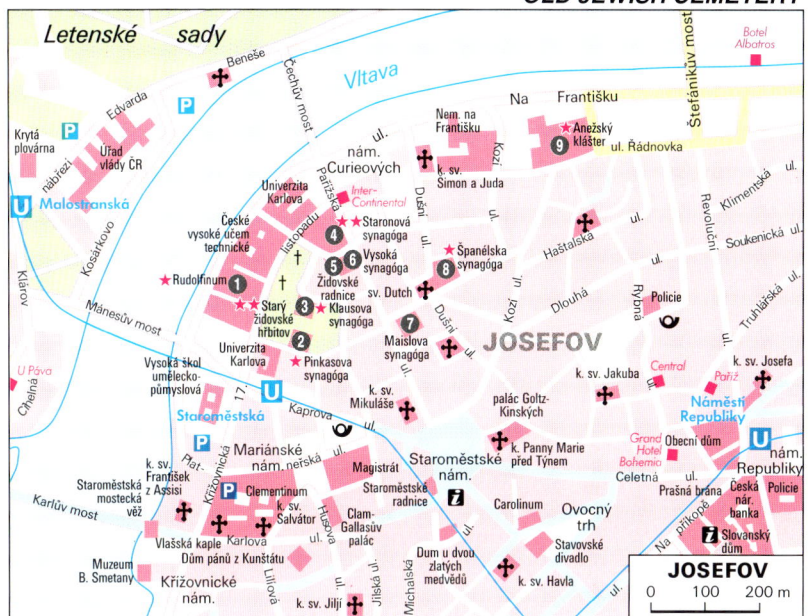

the late 11th and early 12th centuries. Of architectural interest is the cross-ribbed vaulting in the prayer-room, borne by Renaissance struts. The women's gallery, vestibule and meeting room all date from the 17th century.

An important turn of events in the history of the ghetto occurred in 1787 with a prohibition of further burials in the **\*\*Old Jewish Cemetery**. More than 12,000 Gothic, Renaissance and Baroque gravestones have been counted by curators here. Because the Jewish religion prohibits the unearthing of old graves, the dead were, on account of acute lack of space, buried in layers up to twelve deep. This explains the hilly aspect of the cemetery. The tomb inscriptions are all in Hebrew, and contain, in addition to personal data, some lyrical texts such as hymns of praise to the departed. The symbols (bears or deer, hands raised in blessing, grapes, crowns, branches and many more) also allude to the deceased person's name and profession. The area has the feeling of a history book made of

stone, in which the visitor can run through the centuries. In the labyrinth of gravestones, weathered and askew, in the shade of the old deciduous trees are several famous tombs.

The oldest tomb is that of the poet Avigdor Kara, dating from 1439. Rabbi Markus Mordechai Maisl (1528-1601), Mayor of the Jewish quarter and one of the most influential citizens of his time, is buried here; a synagogue and street were named after him. The astronomer and historian David Gans was buried here in 1613. **The tomb of the scholar Rabbi Loew** (1609) is also a pilgrimage site for non-Jews. There is a Jewish ritual of placing a stone on the grave, a tradition dating from when their forefathers left Egypt generations ago, for in the desert, the sandy graves had to be protected. For non-Jews, the gesture is rather more "fashionable" than an actual religious act. Many people also leave lists of requests on Rabbi Loew's tomb; they still believe in the supernatural powers of the creator of the Golem.

The neo-Romanesque **Ceremonial Hall** at the entrance to the Old Cemetery brings the visitor abruptly back into the 20th century: drawings, school books and diaries of children interred in the Theresienstadt (Terezín) concentration camp give chilling insight into the situation of these young Jewish victims of Nazi racism.

### *Cell Synagogue and **Old-New Synagogue

The *Cell Synagogue ❸ (*Klausova synagóga*) derives its name from the tiny cell-like rooms of the Talmud school and the prayer-room. After several restorations and much remodeling over the last 300 years, this synagogue now exhibits old manuscripts and prints and artefacts of Jewish rites and culture.

There was a synagogue here in the 11th century, when the first Jews settled on the Vtlava, in the street known today as

*Above: The early Gothic Old-New Synagogue.*

Široká. Later it was referred to as the Old Synagogue. Today only fragments of this building remain. On this site, the oldest of the ghetto, new synagogues were repeatedly built over the centuries, replacing those which had fallen victim to fire or pogroms.

The early Gothic **Old-New Synagogue ❹ (*Staronová synagóga*), in Red Lane (*Červená*) was built around 1270, and is the only original remaining house of prayer in the ghetto.

Following the Nazi destruction of the synagogue in Worms, the Old-New Synagogue endures as the oldest Jewish house of Prayer in Europe. The Jewish community of Prague still holds services here. Despite later additions, it illustrates what the Ghetto looked like during the Middle Ages. The striking brick gable at the front was added at the end of the 15th century, and the women's gallery was added during the 17th and 18th centuries. The religious objects shimmer in the diffuse light which enters through the small colored windows. The Torah shrine for the five books of the Old Testament, the chancel (called *almemor* in Hebrew) as well as the beautifully-crafted 15th-century grating are particularly noteworthy.

### Jewish Town Hall and High Synagogue

The clock on the neighboring **Jewish Town Hall** ⑤ confuses all those not in the know: the clock with the Hebrew dial runs "backwards": not only is it counter-clockwise, but the big hand shows the hours and the little hand the minutes. This is the location of the administrative seat of Prague's Jewish community as well as the council of the country's Jewish communities, in what is presently the only existing Jewish Town Hall outside of Israel. In the main hall, with its finely-crafted stucco work and ornamental decorations there is now the kosher restaurant *Kosher Shalom*, in which kosher food and drinks are served. Next door is the **High Synagogue** ⑥ (*Vysoká synagóga*), also known as the Town Hall synagogue (1570). Late Gothic elements are mingled with Renaissance ones. The finely worked stucco and the ornaments on the main portal, which were integrated into the renovations of 1883, are particularly noteworthy. Unfortunately, the High Synagogue is no longer open to the public.

### Maisl Synagogue and *Spanish Synagogue

The 16th century **Maisl Synagogue** ⑦ (*Maislova synagóga*) on Maislova No. 10 was built anew at the end of the 19th century. There is an exhibition on the history of the Jews in Bohemia and Moravia presented here. The designs by architect Vojtěch Ignác Ullmann were accepted in 1868 to build a magnificent synagogue in a modern Moorish-Oriental style.

The **\*Spanish Synagogue** ⑧ (*Španělska synagóga*), is a reminder that the Sephardic Jews originally came from the western regions of Europe. The opulently decorated interior enhances the exterior design. It is interesting that the organist here for 12 years was – remarkably for a synagogue – the non-Jewish composer František Škroup, who wrote what would later become the Czech national anthem. Today this synagogue, with its wealth of ornamentation and stucco work, houses an exhibit of religious textiles (Torah wraps, curtains, embroidery, woven material) from over five centuries.

These stem – as do all of the numerous articles in the Jewish Museum – from a collection established in 1906 by Prague Jews. Ironically, the collection was expanded during the Holocaust as Adolf Eichmann "added" to it items from destroyed communities with a view toward establishing a "Museum of an Extinct Race."

### Detour to the *St. Agnes Monastery

Northeast of the Ghetto, close to the Vtlava River, the former **\*St. Agnes Monastery** ⑨ (*Anežský klášter*), is well worth a visit. It is one of the most precious early Gothic buildings in Bohemia, and the first early Gothic edifice in Prague. The building is listed as a national heritage building. The lovely cloisters are of historical interest, for in the 1230s, two orders, the female Poor Clares and the male Minorites (Friars Minor), founded a double monastery here, a virtually unique historical phenomenon.

Next door, in one of the oldest remaining religious complexes of the city, there were once two churches (St. Barbara and St. Francis). These were secularized in the year 1782, and the buildings suffered neglect, and were degraded to warehouses. The extensively renovated buildings house exhibits of the National Gallery, including 19th-century Bohemian painters and sculptors, and temporary exhibits from the collection of the Museum of Decorative Arts.

*Josefov*

# NEW TOWN

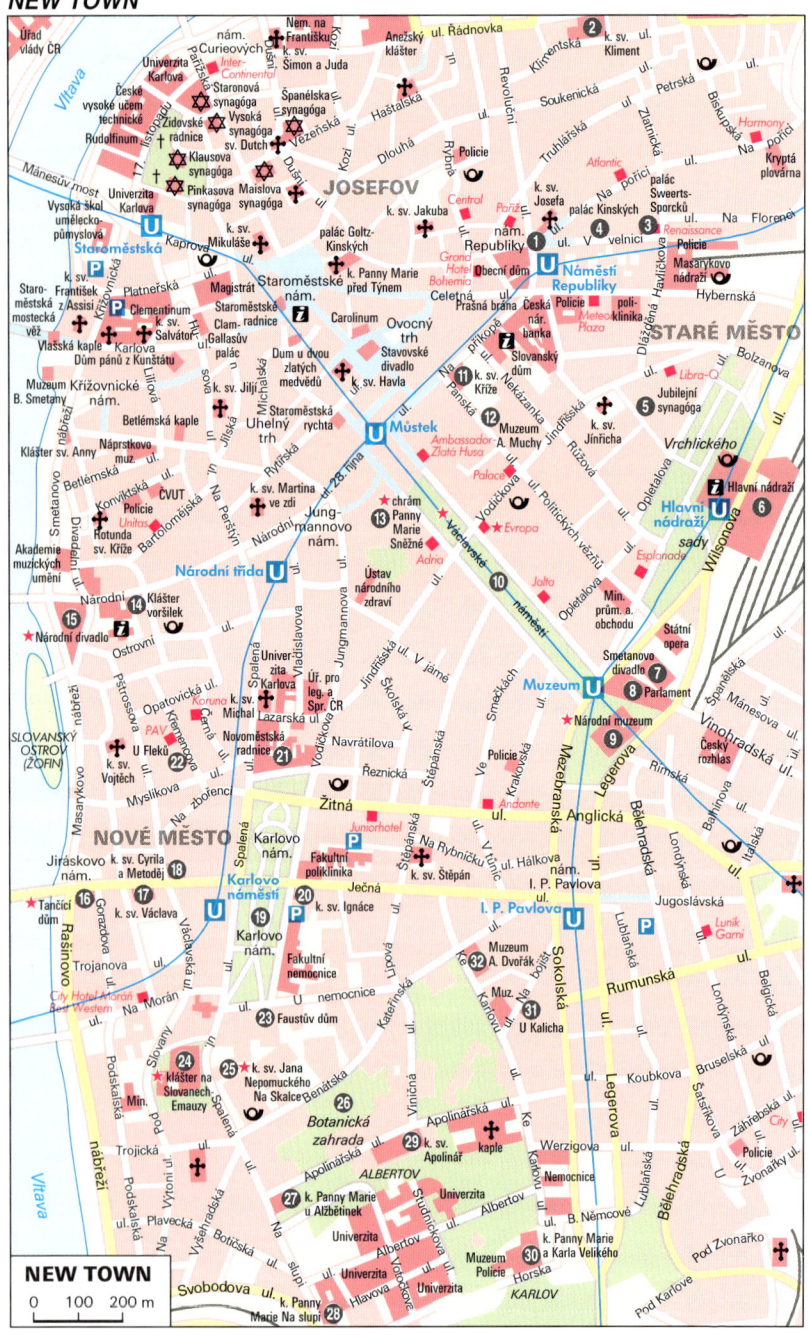

### *NEW TOWN / NOVÉ MĚSTO

Paradoxical as it may sound, Prague's New Town (*Nové Město*) is actually old. It has been in existence for over 650 years. As the Bohemian King Charles IV was also the Holy Roman Emperor, it was imperative that he make a great display of his might and of his glory. He decided to make Prague the capital of his realm. In order to systematically enlarge the over-populated capital on the Vtlava, the Emperor ordered that a new town of Prague be established outside the gates of the Old Town in 1348. The imperial-royal command was unequivocal: "Anyone who receives permission to build must begin construction within one month and must be finished within 18 months." Of course the King did not want to alienate the town councilors of the Old Town, so he granted the Old Town's residents several important privileges. They were to have the right of free passage at all times, and they were even to be responsible for closing and opening two of the New Town's city gates themselves. Charles' offer to resettle in the New Town such Old Town artisans and craftsmen who were "loud" or forced to work in cramped quarters went over well. Thus, many street names clearly refer to this Imperial policy: Blacksmiths' Lane (*Kovářská*), Potters' Lane (*Hrnčířská*), In the Tannery (*V jirchářích*), Furriers' Lane (*Kožišnická*), Clothmakers' Lane (*Soukenická*), Foundry Lane (*Pasířská*), Carpenters' Lane (*Truhlářská*), Ropemakers' Lane (*Provaznická*), Butchers' Lane (*Řeznícká*) or Between the Bakers (*Mezi pekaři*).

### Republic Square and Central Train Station

The visit begins on **Republic Square** ❶ (*Náměstí Republiky*) with a metro station. Two quick detours to the North are well worth it for those interested in history of art. The graphic artist Wenzel Hollar (1607-77) was born in the house at Soukenická ulice 13, while **St. Clemens Church** ❷ (*Kostel svatého Kliment*), belonging to the Protestant Church of the Bohemian Brothers, is in Klimentská.

On Republic Square is the Capuchin church of St. Joseph (*Kostel svatého Josefa*). The former **Sweerts-Sporck Palace** ❸ in Hybernská was remodeled as a bank by Josef Gočár in the 1920s. It was originally built by Anton Hafenecker and Ignazio Palliardi, while Ignaz Platzer the Younger crafted the statues on the facade. In the Middle Ages, this street was an important route into and out of the city. The early Baroque **Kinsky Palace** ❹ in the New Town (not to be confused with the Goltz-Kinsky Palace on the Old Town Ring) was built by Carlo Lurago in Empire style. The palace was remodeled in the first decade of the 20th century and renamed **House of the People** (*Lidový dům*). The Moorish-Oriental **Jubilee Synagogue** ❺ (*Jubilenjí synagóga*), built by the architects W. Stiassny and A. Richter in 1905-06, is located on Jeruzalémská and is still used today by the Jewish Community.

The visitor is advised not to linger in the *Vrchlického* Park for safety reasons (pickpockets, beggars, etc.). The small park borders on the **Central Train Station** ❻ (*Hlvaní nádraží*), named for American President Thomas Wilson. The monumental edifice (architect, J. Fanta) with outsized carved figures was built in the Prague secession style from 1901-09. Continuing along Wilsonova třída towards Wenceslas Square, the visitor catches a glimpse of the **Smetana Theater** ❼, built from 1886-1888 as a neo-Renaissance German Theater.

The master builders were the most highly solicited architects of the time between Hamburg and Odessa: Ferdinand Fellner and Hermann Helmer from Vienna. The State Opera ensemble now performs at the theater, the interior of which is in Neo-Rococo style.

New Town

The **Parliament Buildings** ❽, seat of the former Federal Assembly of the Czechoslovakian Republic, were completed in 1972. The irony of this is that today, Radio Free Europe works in this building.

### Around *Wenceslas Square

The construction of the *National Museum ❾ (*Národní muzeum*), with a facade of over 100 meters in length and with its 700-meter-long gilded cupola, took only five years (1885-90) under the architect Josef Schulz.

The terrace of the museum provides a lovely view of *Wenceslas Square ❿, which is almost 700 meters long. Until the mid-19th century the Horse Gate was located here, the boundary of the traditional Horse Market. Today, the square is

*Above: Art nouveau detail at the Central Train Station – evoking the founding of the Republic on October 28, 1918. Right: Wenceslas Square with the National Museum.*

the pulsing center of the metropolis. The patron saint Wenceslas (Václav), is the most famous and best-loved of all Bohemian national saints. His greater than life-size **equestrian statue** in front of the National Museum was created by Josef Myslbek in 1912-13. The statue is surrounded by saints Ludmilla, Prokop, Agnes and Adalbert. They have borne witness to many events of national importance: it was here that the citizens of the First Czechoslovakian Republic cheered their president Masaryk. In 1939, the German Wehrmacht took possession of the square, as did the united armies of the Warsaw Pact in 1968. In protest against the suppression of the "Prague Spring," student Jan Palach immolated himself here in 1969. In the fall of 1989, peaceful mass demonstrations on Wenceslas Square set the seal upon the end of Socialism in the ČSSR.

On the northern side is the famous *Grand Hotel Europa, one of Prague's art nouveau gems (1889). Unfortunately, the colors of the facade's art nouveau or-

namentation are now somewhat faded. The interior has been maintained as in the original: wood paneling with marquetry inlay, paintings and lovely chandeliers. The Hotel Europa is a favorite movie set on account of its special atmosphere; in addition, it houses one of Prague's most attractive coffee houses.

*Můstek* ("little bridge") is what the inhabitants of Prague call the much-frequented area where one formerly had to cross the trench (*Na příkopě*) from the Old Town to the Horse Market – today's Wenceslas Square. The pedestrian zone of **Na příkopě** tempts with its galleries, department stores, souvenir and delicatessen shops, cafes, book stores and restaurants. The **Sylva-Taroucca Palace** (No. 10), one of Prague's loveliest palaces, was built by Kilian Ignaz Dientzenhofer (1743-51), and later expanded by Anselmo Lurago.

On the corner of Panská is the only Empire church in Prague, the **Holy Cross Church** ⑪ (*Kostel svatého Kříže*, 1816-1824). The Kaunitz Palace (Panská 7) houses the **Alfons Mucha Museum** ⑫ (*Muzeum A. Muchy;* cf page 74). Back to the trench, the visitor quickly comes across the late 18th-century **Slavic House** (*Slovanský dům*), with a ČEDOK information office and several restaurants.

On ul. 28 října one arrives from the opposite side of the Můstek at the sweet *Jungmannovo náměstí*, a small oasis amongst the hustle and bustle of the metropolis. The Gothic **★Church of the Virgin Mary of the Snow** ⑬ (*chrám Panny Marie Sněžné*) already dominated the scene of the New Town at the time of Charles IV. It is the second-largest House of God in Prague. Planned to be larger than St. Vitus Cathedral, the Hussite War prevented its completion. The church's altar is also a superlative: it is the tallest altar in Prague (30 meters).

The New Town is divided from the Old Town, both historically and administratively, by **Národní třída**, or National Boulevard. The name of this boulevard set the tone for a truly "new" wind blowing through Prague after it became the

capital of a new nation in 1918: a new sense of self-respect was evident in a city which the Hapsburgs had "demoted" to the status of a mere royal residence, which Prague residents took as a real put-down. The National Boulevard was laid down over the former trench, and, with its numerous edifices dating from the 18th, 19th and 20th century, is one of Prague's most magnificent streets.

On the corner of Jungmannova is the striking Renaissance-style **Adria Palace**, from the years 1923-25. It was formerly the seat of an Italian insurance company. Just before the Vtlava Quay is the Baroque **Ursuline Convent** ⑭ (*klášter voršilek*) and its church of the same name. The interior of the church is magnificent. The statues are by F. Preiss. Peter Brandl painted the main altarpiece, *The Assumption of the Virgin Mary* and the ceiling frescoes are by Johann Jakob Steinfels. The sculpture group of John of Nepomu-

cene in front of the monastery buildings was created by Ignaz Platzer the Elder (1747). It is cozy in the monastery's tradition-steeped wine tavern (*klášterní vinárna*). On the northern side of the street is the magnificently restored Topič Publishing House (No. 9) as well as the art nouveau former seat of an insurance company (No. 7).

The *****National Theater** ⑮ (*Národní divadlo*) was an outlet for the Czech population's desire, long before the turn of the century, to have their own voice within the German-language center of Prague. The tones emanating from the theater (designed by Josef Zítek and Josef Schulz) were also new: Smetana's national opera, *Libuše,* was staged in 1883 at the theater's reopening (the first building burned down in 1881). Today, the National Theater is still the pride of the city, a gilded wonder created by the most important artists of that era. Proudly the inscription over the entrance proclaims, "Narod sobě" (The nation unto itself). The **Café Slavia** opposite tempts the visi-

*Above: In the National Theater. Right: The Dancing House on Rašinovo nábřeží.*

*New Town*

tor to enter (cf page 78). On tumultuous and loud Vtlava Quay, continue walking upriver for a while. On the southern tip of the **Slavic Island** (*Slovanský ostrov*) is **Manés House** with a famous exhibition of modern art.

### Around Charles Square

Close to the Vtlava, on the corner of Rašínovo nábřeží / Jiráskovo nám., the *Dancing House ⑯ (Tančicí dům) has been attracting attention since 1996. The twin towers nestling closely together are supposed to represent the famous dancing duo of Ginger (Rogers) and Fred (Astaire). The transparent wire ball on the right-hand tower evokes the style of secession pavilions in Vienna. Many world-famous architects, such as Frank O. Gehry and Eva Jiřičná, a London architect of Bohemian extraction, participated in this project, which was to fill an ugly hole left when a building was torn down. The customer was a Dutch insurance company, the *National Nederlanden.* To-

day, there are offices here, as well as the bar, *Le Valence,* which is on the ground floor; and the luxurious French restaurant, *La Perle de Prague,* which occupies the upper story.

Large Romanesque fragments can be seen in the Gothic **Wenceslas Church ⑰** (*Kostel svatého Václava*). The Gothic-era frescoes in the presbytery date from around 1400. Today, the church known as **St. Cyril and St. Methodius Church ⑱** (*Kostel svatého Cyrila a Metoděj*), built in 1730-36 by Kilian Ignaz Dientzen-hofer, is the seat of the local Orthodox congregation. The church is remembered as the site of the last stand of the group of parachutists who, in 1942, assassinated the despised Nazi official, Imperial Protector Heydrich. Following their denunciation, the church was flooded and the hunted committed suicide. Bouquets are still placed there in honor of these heroes.

**Charles Square ⑲** (*Karlovo náměstí*) is the largest enclosed square in Prague. A church there dedicated to **St. Ignatius of Loyola ⑳** (*Kostel svatého Ignáce*)

served as the seat of the New Town Jesuits until their order was disbanded. Carlo Lurago selected a lavish mixture of Baroque and Rococo elements for this church (1665-77). Visible from afar is the statue of the saint, with a halo, which dates from 1671.

The national landmark *Novoměstská radnice*, the **Town Hall of the New Town** ㉑, has been renovated repeatedly since the 14th century, and extensively so in 1905. Its tower has managed to preserve its mid-15th century appearance. The first Defenestration of Prague took place in this Town Hall on July 30, 1419; adherents of the reformer Jan Hus hurled Catholic officials from the window – into the midst of an angry mob. On Charles Square in front of the Town Hall, with its many statues of Czech writers, scientists and artists, it is easy to forget that just a century and a half ago wood, coal, live-

stock and salt herring were traded here. At the time, the New Town had a monopoly on the sale of herring. The former character of this district is also apparent in the street names *Ječná* (Barley Lane) and *Žitná* (Grain Lane). Still, it's astounding to learn that there were, during that period, some 150 pubs on this square and in the surrounding area. This is a vivid illustration of the fact that, then as now, the Czechs are among the leading consumers of beer in the world.

Beer drinkers from all over the world will enjoy a visit to the Old Czech beer parlor **U FlekŮ** ㉒ in the near by Křemcová 11. The famous black 13-% ale with a hint of caramel has been flowing from these tradition-steeped premises since 1499. A large clock hangs over the entrance. The neo-Gothic halls seat 450 thirsty people. The malting house was formerly located in the Knight's Hall. The 500 places in the shady beer garden quickly fill up when the weather is fine.

The **Faust House** ㉓ (*Faustův dům*) is at the south end of Charles Square. Tradi-

*Above: The U FlekŮ beer garden, steeped in tradition.*

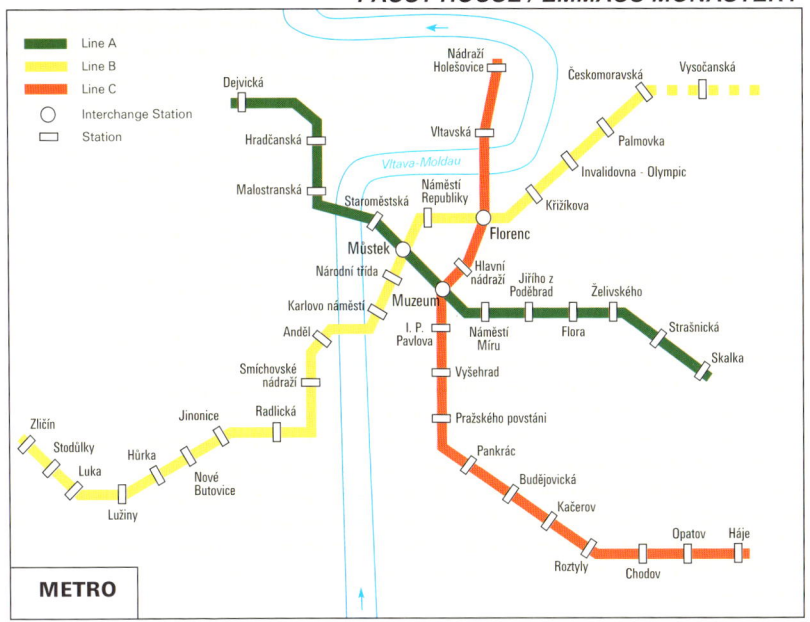

New Town

tion has it that mysterious creatures dwell in this 16th-century Renaissance building with its Baroque elements. The first of these was Englishman Edward Kelley, who claimed he could manufacture gold. Emperor Rudolph II ordered him to Prague in the 17th century. Following the death of his patron, the unfortunate man was thrown into the dungeons by the successor to the throne, King Matthew. Chemist Mladota experimented in this house at the beginning of the 18th century. Faust is said to have lived here and legend has it that he went straight to Hell from here upon his death.

The **\*Emmaus monastery** ㉔ (*Klášter na Slovanech-Emauzy*) to the South was founded by Charles IV in 1347 for Slavic Benedictine monks. It was named thus because the scripture lesson "Jesus' encounter with the disciples in Emmaus" was read at its consecration. Services in this church were popular because they were held not in Latin, but in Old Church Slavic. The church changed hands numerous times; its owners ranged from the congregation of the Hussite brothers to Spanish Benedictines. The entire complex was given its Baroque face-lift in the mid-17th century; around 1880, German Benedictines from Beuron renovated it in neo-Gothic style. The church's rather extravagant appearance today, however, is a result of renovations undertaken in the 1960's. Today, the cloister of this national landmark houses the Institutes of the Czech Academy of Science.

Not far away is one of the most beautiful of Kilian Ignaz Dientzenhofer's churches: the rarely-visited **\*Church of St. John of Nepomucene on the Rock** ㉕ (*Kostel svatého Jana Nepomuckého Na Skalce*), built between 1730-39. The wooden statue of its patron saint was carved by Johann Brokoff (1682).

In the **Botanical Gardens** ㉖ (*Botanická zahrada*) the visitor can stroll and bide for a time before continuing on the sightseeing tour.

The church of **Our Lady Mary in the Elizabethan Convent** ㉗ (*Kostel Panny Marie u Alžbětinek*) is the work of Kilian

Ignaz Dientzenhofer (1724-25). The frescoes in the adjacent **St. Thecla Chapel** are by Johann Lukas Kracker (around 1762). The Elizabethan Convent was originally Baroque but was modernized in the 1930s.

The Servite church **Our Lady Mary of the Pillar** ㉘ (*Kostel Panny Marie Na slupi*) dates from the 14th century, while its neo-Gothic monastery is from 1858.

The chapter house of the **Church of St. Apollinaris** ㉙ houses the Psychiatry Department of Charles University; this single-nave Gothic church was built in 1390, during the reign of Charles IV, and its frescoes date from the same period.

The **Church of Our Lady and Charlemagne** ㉚ (*Kostel Panny Marie a Karla Velikého*) was consecrated in 1377 in honor of the patron saint of the Emperor and King. This oft-remodeled church has been a popular place of pilgrimage since the 18th century.

The *Tavern U Kalicha* (**House of the Jug**) ㉛, located on *Na Bojišti* (On the Battlefield), is the site of many key scenes in the immortal anti-war novel *The Good Soldier Švejk*. In this book by the Prague humorist Jaroslav Hašek (1883-1923), the rheumatic dog dealer Josef Švejk carries out his battle of wits against the imperial army with naiveté and cleverness, with innocence and flair. A true literary monument!

A gem by Kilian Ignaz Dientzenhofer, this time a secular structure, is the Pleasure Palace of Count Michna (*Letohrádek Michnů*), built between 1712-20, also called "Villa America." Today it houses the **Antonín Dvořák Museum** ㉜. The frescoes are by J.F. Schor, while the statues are from the workshop of Matthias B. Braun. Dvořák (1841-1904), who lived at Žitná ulice 14 from 1877 until his death, is, along with Smetana, the most important and most popular Czech composer. The museum in the Michna Palace exhibits a cross-section of his life and work.

## PRAGUE (☎ 02)

The Prague Information Service, **PIS**, has several branches. There are also countless private agents who approach visitors along the "tourist mile" (Wenceslas Square – Na Příkopě – Celetná – Staroměstské náměstí – Karlova – Charles Bridge – Mostecká). The Czech name of Wenceslas Square, Václavské náměstí is used for accommodation listings.

**PIS**, all the following branches are in Prague 1 (P-1), Na Příkopě 20, Tel. 264022-3; Staroměstské náměstí 1, Tel. 24482018; Malostranská Mostecká věž, Tel. 536010; Hlavní nádraží (main railway station), in the ticket hall, Tel. 24239258. All the PIS offices can be called under the phone numbers Tel. 187 or 544444. Internet: www. prague-info.cz or www.pis.cz Click on the British flag to get the English translation.

**ČEDOK**, P-1, Na Příkopě 18, Tel. 2419 7615, Fax 24210502, www.cedok.cz

*PRIVATE AGENCIES:* **AVE**, P-2, Wilsonova 8, Tel. 24223226, 24223521, Fax 24223463, e-mail: ave@avetravel.cz; **Martin Tour**, P-1, Štěpánská 61, Tel. / Fax 24212473. **Pragotur**, P-1, Za Poříčskou branou 7, Tel. 24816120, Fax 24816172. **Top Tour**, P-1, Rybná 3, Tel. 2321077, Fax 24811400. **Universitas Tour**, P-1, Opletalova 38, Tel. 260426, Fax 24212290.

*AUTO:* Taking a car into the center of Prague is not recommended. Streets are narrow and congested, public garages expensive. The police will block cars in violation of the parking laws.

**Attended parking**: P-1: Wilsonova (at the main railway station / Hlavní nádraží), V Celnici, Malostranské nám., Na Florenci (at the Masaryk station), Těšnov (at the Ministry of Agriculture). P-2: Škrétova, nám. Míru, Tylovo nám.

*TRAIN AND BUS TRANSPORTATION:* **Main Railway Station** (Hlavní nádraží), P-2, Wilsonova 8, Metro (subway) line C (between the Metro stations Muzeum and Florenc). Other train stations: **Nadraží Holešovice**, Partysánská (Metro C). **Masarykovo nádraží**, Hybernská (Metro B), **Smíchovské nádraží**, Nádražní (Metro B). **Bus stations**: Florenc, P-8, Na Florenci (Metro B, C to the station called Florenc). Smíchov, P-5, Na Knížecí (Metro B to Anděl). Roztyly, P-4, Ryšavého (Metro C to Roztyly). Holešovice, P-7, Partyzánská (Metro C to Nádraží Holešovice).

*SUBWAYS, TRAMS, BUSES:* For information see www. dp-praha.cz, subway plan page 59. The "Metro" (M) system includes three subway lines (A, green), (B, yellow) and (C, red). They are supplemented by a network of trams and bus lines in the city. Suburbs can be reached by buses departing from the city center or from various other streets and subway stations. Night buses and trams run midnight- 5:00 a.m. The funicular (standing room only) to the top of **Lawrence Mountain** (Petřin Hill) runs daily between 9:15 a.m. and 8:45 p.m. and can be reached by trams 9, 12 and 22. (lower station at Újezd / Lesser Town). The same tickets are valid for all local transportation. All Metro stations have an "automat" where you can buy single ride tickets; five Metro stations also have information centers where single, full-day, and multiple-day tickets can be purchased. Tobacco shops, news stands, travel bureaus, many restaurants, hotel reception desks, and groceries also sell tickets. Subway tickets must be canceled in special machines before going down to the platform. For the bus and train, the canceling machine is inside the vehicle; cancel the ticket immediately after boarding. Tickets with various periods of validity are available: the standard ticket is valid for one hour (off-peak 90 minutes) and you can transfer between types of transportation. Tickets for a shorter ride (funicular, night buses, night trams excluded) allow either 15 minutes on the bus or tram or a distance of four stops (within 30 minutes) on the subway, but no transfers are permitted. For tourists and others who use the system heavily, there are full-day and multiple-day tickets, allowing unlimited travel and transfers on the day(s) the ticket is valid (multiple: choice of 3, 7, or 15 days). Children under six ride free; from six to fifteen at childrens' prices. The tickets are inexpensive and riders caught without a valid ticket must pay a steep fine.

*TAXIS:* Taxis are easy to find and inexpensive by western standards, if you insist on the local rates before beginning the ride (cf "Travel Information, Taxis", p. 92).

*BOATS:* Information about water transportation on the Vtlava is available at the Palacký Bridge (*Palackého most*): P-2, Rašínovo nábřeží, Tel. 298309, 293803, Fax 24913862. In the summer months, the **Prague Steamboat Company** offers excursions to Barrandov and Vyšehrad, to the zoo, to Roztoky and to the Slapy dam.

*CITY TOURS:* **PIS** (P-1, Na Příkopě 20, Tel. 187 and 544444); **Prague Sightseeing Tours**, P-1, Klimentská 52, Tel. 2314661; e-mail: pst@mbox.vol.cz; **Prague Walks**, P-2, Nezamyslova 7, Tel. 61214603 (walking tours with various themes, for example, traces of the Velvet Revolution, "Ghosts of Prague"); **Green & Gold**, P-4, Počátecká 13, Tel. 61262498; **DC Service**, P-1, Pařížská 10, Tel. 2325420, e-mail: info@dc-service.com; **La Bohème Tours**, P-6, Závěrka 4/412, Tel. 33116111, Fax 33116222, e-mail: sales@la-boheme.cz. Tourists who would like to explore the streets of Prague from a small train should check out **Ekoexpres**, P-2, Slezská 11, Tel. 253159, Fax 253159. The tour begins approximately on the hour on the Old Town Ring behind the Hus Memorial. **Pony Travel**, Tel./Fax 295641 arranges rides in pony cabs, from the Old Town Ring and other departure points.

A tour by observation car is offered by **Novum Tour**: P-1, Vaclavské náměstí 21, Tel. 24235097, Fax 24239065. **Martin Tour** offers, in addition to city tours, **boat excursions** and **observation flights** in its program: P-1, Štěpánská 61, Tel. 24212473. To see Prague from a **hot air balloon**, contact the **Prague Tourist Ballooning Company**, P-2, Sokolská 19, Tel. 295833, Fax 295878.

**Main Post Office** (*Hlavní poštovní úřad*), Jindřišská 14, Tel. 21131445. Post office with 24-hour service: P-1, Hybernská 13, Tel. 2422 5845. Post office with customs clearance: P-5, Plzeňská 139, Tel. 57019111. Post office with fax capabilities: P-1, Politických vězňů 4, Fax 24215146.

**Emergencies:** Tel. 155, **Ambulance** (non-emergency): Tel. 67313333. **Pharmacies with after-hours service** (several): P-1, Palackého 5, Tel. 24946982; P-2, Belgická 37, Tel. 258189; P-4, Anny Drabíkové 534, Tel. 7912743. **After-hours Medical Consultation** (several): P-1, Palackého 5, Tel. 24949181; P-2, Sokolská 27, Tel. 299676; P-3, Koněvova 205, Tel. 6848685; P-4, Pocovská 31, Tel. 90057917; P-5, Roentgenova 2, Na Homolce Hospital, Tel. 52922146. **After-hours Dental Clinic:** P-1, Palackého 5, Tel. 24946981 (Mon-Fri 7:00 p.m. to 7:00 a.m., Sat, Sun 24-hour service).

Cash and traveler's checks should be exchanged only in **banks** (for example, at the **Komerční banka**), official currency exchange outlets (*směnarna*), or at such outlets as **American Express** and **Thomas Cook**. If no commission is charged, the exchange rate offered is probably unfavorable. The commissions charged by banks should not exceed 2 %. The exchange rate in hotels is generally unfavorable. Traveler's checks are not generally accepted by restaurants, shops, etc. Well-known **credit cards** are generally accepted.

Telephone and Fax numbers are constantly changing. When in doubt, try International Directory Assistance or the Czech Yellow Pages in the Internet (www.mediatel.cz). In the following listings, the borders of the various neighborhoods in the city are not observed scrupulously, and in a few instances hotels close to each other are listed in separate sections.

**"Botels"** are an invention from the socialist days, a way of addressing the undersupply of tourist accommodation. They are actually hotels on the Vltava which have the appearance and character of boats, but were never used as such. A large number of agents specialize in finding accommodations for tourists in **private homes**. The Prague Information Service (PIS) and the travel agency Čedok also offer this service. Local people wishing to rent out rooms in their homes, or hawkers representing them, often seek out tourists right at the railway stations.

*New Town*

# PRAGUE DOWNTOWN

**Youth Hostels** – the booking office **CKM**, P-2, Žitná 10-12, Tel. 291240-221, open 9:00 a.m. to 6:00 p.m, near Karlova; arranges the cheapest accommodations in Prague for young, easy-to-please tourists. During the breaks between university semesters, rooms are also available in the student housing behind the Petřín.

🚫 Pitching a tent just anywhere is not permitted. In the heart of the city there are no camping grounds. The outlying city sections do offer **camping grounds** and **trailer parks** as follows: PRAGUE 4: **Intercamp Kotva**, U Ledáren 55, Tel. 461712, 466085, Fax 466110, open mid-April to October, in the South between the Vltava and a sports club. Offers tennis court and bicycle rental, Is convenient to the expressway. PRAGUE 5: **Eva**, Strojírenská 78, Tel. 3019213, flat meadow with fruit trees. **Caravancamp**, Plzeňska 279, Tel. 524714, terraced meadow with trees on the hill, tram nearby. **Sportcamp**, Nad Hliníkem 2, Tel. 521802, Fax 521632, tennis court available, located 700 m from a tram stop. **Karavan Park Císařská louka**, Císařská louka 599, Tel. 545064, Fax 543305, trailer park on an island in the Vltava. PRAGUE 6: **Džbán** (SK Aritma), Nad Lávkou 3, Tel. 368551, Fax 361365, also offers indoor accommodation, tennis court, sauna, fitness room, small reservoir, close to the beautiful Šárka Gorge, tram nearby. PRAGUE 7 (Troja): **Sokol Troja**, Trojská 171a, Tel. 6881 177, open year-round, flat meadow surrounded by trees and bushes. Additional campsites on Trojská are the **Autocamp Hájek** and **Trojská**, both of which offer indoor accommodation. From Troja there are good bus connections to the city center. PRAGUE 8: **Na Vlachovce**, Zenklova 217, Tel. 6880214, also indoor accommodation, tram stop nearby. **Triocamp**, Obslužná 43, Tel. 6881180, meadow with trees, bus and tram connections. **Busek**, U Parku 6, Tel. / Fax 8591852, meadow with hedges, tennis court, sauna, accessible by bus and tram. PRAGUE 9: **Tj Sokol Dolní Počernice**, Národních hrdinů 290, Tel. 727501, on the banks of a pond, with tennis court, served by bus and Metro. **Siesta**, Pod Šancemi 5, Tel. 821423, bus and tram.

## CASTLE DISTRICT AND LESSER TOWN

🏨 ⭐⭐⭐ **Savoy**, P-6, Keplerova 6, Tel. 24302430, Fax 24311218, e-mail: savhoprg@mbox.vol.cz, upon request, a room with your own butler. Close to the Castle. **Diplomat**, P-6, Evropská 15, Tel. 24394111, Fax 24394215, meets western hotel standards, handicapped accessible, swimming pool, sauna, fitness center, close to the Metro. **Hoffmeister**, P-1, Pod Bruskou 9, Tel. 57310942, Fax 57320906, e-mail: hotel@hoffmeister.cz **U Tří pštrosů**, P-1, Dražického náměstí 12, Tel. 57320565, Fax 57320611, in a historic former ruin right at the Charles Bridge, with its usual bustle, traffic, noise.

⭐⭐ **U Páva**, P-1, U Lužického semináře 32, Tel. 57320743, Fax 533379, comparable to the U Tří pštrosů, but quieter. **Kampa – Stará zbrojnice**, P-1, Všehrdova 16, Tel. 57320404, Fax 57320262, in a former weapons arsenal, renovated, plain and functional, on a quiet side street. ⭐ **U Raka**, P-1, Černínská 1093, Tel. 20514792, Fax 20510511, classy, renovated, with romantic garden, close to the Castle.

🏛 **Prague Castle** (*Pražský hrad*): daily 5:00 a.m. – 12:00 midnight, Nov-Mar to 11:00 p.m. Exhibition rooms open daily 9:00 a.m. to 5:00 p.m., Nov-Mar to 4:00 p.m., www.hrad.cz. **Castle Gardens**: Apr-Sep daily 10:00 a.m. – 6:00 p.m. **Loreto Church**, Loretánské nám. 7, Tues-Sun 9:00 a.m – 12:15 p.m. and 1:00 – 4:30 p.m. **Strahov Monastery** (*Strahovský klášter*), Strahovské dvůr 1, treasures from the Gothic through the Romantic periods, Tues-Sun 9:00 a.m. – 12:00 noon and 1:00 – 5:00 p.m.

*LESSER TOWN (MALÁ STRANA):* **Lesser Town Bridge Tower** (*Malostranské mostecké věže*), Charles Bridge, Apr-Oct 10:00 a.m. – 6:00 p.m. **Vrtba Garden** (*Vrtbovská zahrada*), Karmelitská 18, Apr-Oct 10:00 a.m. – 6:00 p.m. **Church of Our Lady Victorious** (*Kostel Panny Marie Vitezné*), Karmelitská 9, Mon-Fri 8:30 a.m. – 6:30 p.m., Sat, Sun to 8:00 p.m. **Lobkowicz Palace (German Embassy)**, Vlašská 19, visits by appointment. Tel. 57113111. **Wallenstein Palace** (*Valdštejnský palác*), Valdštejnské nám. 4, government building, open only for concerts and exhibitions. **Wallenstein Garden** (*Valdštejnská zahrada*), Letenská ul., June-Aug 9:00 a.m. – 7:00 p.m., Apr, May, Sep, Oct 10:00 a.m. – 6:00 p.m. **St. Nicholas Church** (*Kostel svatého Mikuláše*), Malostranské nám., 9:00 a.m. – 5:00 p.m., bell tower Apr-Oct 10:00 a.m. – 6:00 p.m. **Observation Tower on the Petřín** (*Petřínská rozhledna*) and **Labyrinth** (*bludiště*), Petřínské sady, Apr-Aug 10:00 a.m. – 7:00 p.m., Sep and Oct to 6:00 p.m., Nov-Mar only Sat, Sun 10:00 a.m. – 5:00 p.m.

## OLD TOWN AND JOSEFOV

🏨 ⭐⭐⭐ **Inter-Continental**, P-1, náměstí Curieových 43/5, Tel. 24881111, Fax 24811216, e-mail: prague@interconti.com, grand, offers lovely views, fitness room, swimming pool, sauna, handicapped accessible. Near the Jewish Museum. **Grand Hotel Bohemia**, P-1, Králodvorská 4, Tel. 24804111, Fax 2329545, very comfortable, its banquet hall "Boccaccio," in neo-rococo style was used as a film setting. Close to the Powder Tower. **Paříž**, P-1, U Obecního domu 1, Tel. 24222151, 22195195, Fax 2422 5475, e-mail: prgparcz@mbox.vol.cz, considered to be Prague's most beautiful Art Nouveau hotel, stylish cafe. **Renaissance Prague Hotel**, P-1, V Celnici 7, Tel. 21822100, Fax 21822200, modern, swimming pool, sauna, fitness room. 😊😊 **Meteor Plaza**, P-1, Hybernská 6, Tel. 24192111, Fax 24213005, formerly known as "Zur Stadt Wien," imperial lodgings, features a wine bar from the 14th century. **Central**, P-1, Rybná 8, Tel. 24812041, Fax 2328404, near the Jewish Museum. **U Zlatého koníčka**, P-1 Husova 18, Tel. 24009459, Fax 24009299, renovated, reservations are absolutely necessary because this hotel is centrally located and thus much in demand. **Albatros** (Botel), P-1, nábřeží L. Svobody, Tel. 24810547, Fax 24811214, not for guests who are sensitive to noise, or claustrophobic. 😊 **Unitas**, P-1, Bartolomějská 9, Tel. 2327651, simple and clean; alcohol is forbidden on premises.

*YOUTH HOSTELS:* **Travellers Hostel**, P-1, Dlouhá 33, Tel. 24826662, Fax 24826665, e-mail: hostel@travellers.cz, www.travellers.cz With kitchen, bar, Internet access, television, washing machine, luggage room.

🏛 *OLD TOWN:* **Powder Tower** (*Prašná brána*), Na příkopé, Apr-Oct 10:00 a.m. – 6:00 p.m. **Municipal House** (*Obecní dům*), nám. Republiky 5, sightseeing visits by appointment (Tel. 22002100), also houses restaurants and a cafe. **Týn Church** (*Kostel Panny Marie před Týnem*), Staroměstské nám. **Old Town Hall** (*Staroměstské radnice*) with view from the tower, Staroměstské nám. 1, Apr-Oct Mon 11:00 a.m. – 6:00 p.m., Tues-Sun 9:00 a.m. – 6:00 p.m., Nov-Mar to 5:00 p.m. **Carolinum**, Železná 9, Main building of the Charles University with preserved original alcove. **Clam-Gallas Palace** (*Clam-Gallasův palác*), Husova 20, used as a concert hall, otherwise not open to the public. **Holy Cross Rotunda** (*Rotunda svatého kříže*), Karoliny Svetlé. **Bethlehem Chapel** (*Betlémská kaple*), Betlémské nám., Apr-Oct daily 9:00 a.m. – 6:00 p.m., Nov-Mar to 5:00 p.m. **Clementinum**, Mariánské nám. 4, Seat of the National Library, not open for tourist visits, accessible only with library card. The Chapel of Mirrors can be visited only in conjunction with concert attendance. **Old Town Bridge Tower** (*Staroměstská mostecká věž*), Charles Bridge, Apr-Sep 10:00 a.m. – 7:30 p.m., March and October to 6:00 p.m., Nov-Feb to 5:00 p.m.

*JOSEFOV (FORMER JEWISH QUARTER):* **Pinkas Synagogue**, Široká ul., **Maisl Synagogue**, Maislova 10, **Klaus Synagogue**, U starého hřbitova 4, **Spanish Synagogue**, Vézeňská 1, the **Old Jewish Cemetery**, Široká ul., and **Ceremonial Hall** all are part of the **Jewish Museum**, www.jewishmuseum.cz Entrance tickets: U starého hřbitova 3a, Tel. 2317191. The tickets are valid for all the sights belonging to the Jewish Museum. For the **Old-New Synagogue**, Červená ul., a separate entrance fee is levied. The sights of Josefov are open April through October from 9:00 a.m. to 6:00 p.m. and November through March from 9:00 a.m. to 4:30 p.m.,

daily except Saturdays and Jewish holidays. **St. Agnes Monastery** (*Anēzký klášter*) Anežská 12, now houses the seat of the National Gallery, Tues-Sun 10:00 a.m. – 6:00 p.m.

## LOWER (EAST) NEW TOWN

🏨 😊😊😊 **Esplanade**, P-1, Washingtonova 19, Tel. 24211715, Fax 24229306, traditional, comfortable, close to Wenceslas Square, Thomas Mann was a guest here. **Jalta**, P-1, Václavské náměstí 45, Tel. 2422 9133, Fax 24213866, e-mail: jalta@jalta.cz, for nostalgia buffs of the pre-November era, formerly the elegant hotel of prominent artists, recently renovated. **Palace**, P-1, Panská 12, Tel. 24093111, Fax 24221240, e-mail: palhoprg@mbox.vol. cz, Art Nouveau facade, interior modern and plain, sauna, near Wenceslas Square. **Adria**, P-1, Václavské náměstí 26, Tel. 21081111, Fax 21081300, functional. **Ambassador – Zlatá Husa**, Václavské náměstí 5-7, Tel. 24193111, 24218104, Fax 2422 6167, e-mail: ambassad@mbox.vol.cz, traditional house, modernized.

😊😊 **Atlantic**, P-1, Na Poříčí 9, Tel. 24811084, Fax 24812378, pleasant atmosphere. **Harmony**, P-1, Na Poříčí 31, Tel. 2320016, Fax 2310009, renovated. **Evropa**, P-1, Václavské náměstí 25, Tel. 24228117-9, Fax 24224544, beautiful, rather fastidious Art Nouveau hotel, interior would make a lovely film setting. For tolerant nostalgia buffs. **Juliš**, P-1, Václavské náměstí 22, Tel. 24217092, Fax 2421 8545, very well maintained, close to the night life.

😊 **Yaha**, P-1, Václavské náměstí 64, Tel./Fax 2421 6399. **Junior Hotel Praha**, P-1, Senovážné nám. (near main railway station), Tel. 24231754, Fax 24221579. **Libra-Q Hostel**, P-1, Senovážné nám. 21, Tel. 24231754, Fax 24221579. All three are basic and inexpensive.

🏛 **Church of the Virgin Mary of the Snows** (*Chrám Panny Marie Sněžné*), Jungmannovo nám., daily 6:00 a.m. – 7:30 p.m.

## UPPER (SOUTH) NEW TOWN

🏨 😊😊😊 **City Hotel Moráň Best Western**, P-2, Na Moráni 15, Tel. 24915208, Fax 297533, e-mail: bw-moran@login.cz, historic building, under Austrian management. 😊 **Páv**, Křemencova 13, P-1, Tel. 2491 3286, Fax 24910574, small and cozy. **U Melounu**, P-2, Ke Karlovu 7/457, Tel. 24918322, unpretentious and reasonably priced.

🏛 **Orthodox Church of St. Cyril and St. Methodius** (*Kostel svatého Cyrila a Metodēj*), Resslova 9, May-Sep Tues-Sun 10:00 a.m. – 5:00 p.m., Apr-Oct to 4:00 p.m. **New Town Hall** (*Novoměstská radnice*), Karlovo nám. 23, Tues-Sun 10:00 a.m. – 6:00 p.m., Town Hall Tower May-Sep 10:00 a.m. – 6:00 p.m. **Emmaus Monastery** (*Klášter na Slovanech-Emauzy*), Vyšehradská 49, daily except Monday, 9:00 a.m. – 5:00 p.m.

*New Town* (side label)

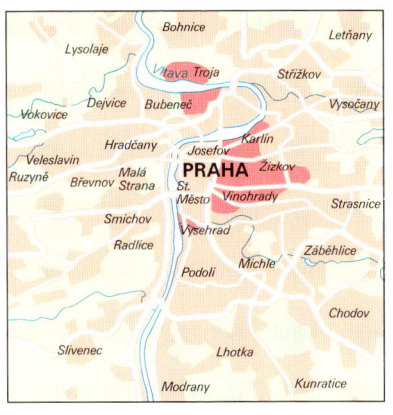

# EXCURSIONS IN AND AROUND PRAGUE

## VYŠEHRAD
## ŽIŽKOV
## TROJA
## KARLŠTEJN

### *VYŠEHRAD

Hradčany Castle was not the only castle in Prague. Up-river from Prague, on a promontory jutting over the Vtlava's left bank, a neo-Gothic church of blackened stone towers over an entire city district. According to legend, Prague's first fortress stood on this cliff. It was known as **\*Vyšehrad**, the "upper castle," said to have been home to the legendary patron figure of the city, Libussa (Libuše).

Vyšehrad replaced Hradčany as sovereign's residence between 1070 and 1140 because of a dispute between the Duke of Bohemia, Vratislav II (who became King Vratislav I in 1085) and his brother Jaromír, Bishop of Prague, who was head of the Church in Prague. Vratislav, who had been installed as the representative of Rome by the Emperor, claimed Prague's episcopal seat for himself. As he was unable to win out over his brother, however, he proceeded to establish his own cathedral branch on Vyšehrad, where he felt he held power simply by virtue of the authority vested in him by Rome.

After 1140, the castle began to decline in significance and fall into decay. Not until Charles IV came to power did it gain

*Left: The Karlštejn Castle crowns a 320-meter-high limestone cliff.*

renewed strategic importance as a means of protection for the New Town, which he founded in 1348. The walls of Vyšehrad were joined with the new walls being constructed around the city. Nine churches were built within the fortress, manned with 100 priests. During the first Hussite war, the army of the Reformation attacked this bulwark of Catholicism in 1420, destroying all of the buildings except St. Martin's Rotunda and the Church of Saint Peter and Saint Paul.

In the 17th century, the fortress was renovated for the last time, and expanded into a Baroque bastion. The last fortification element, a large brick gate (*Cihelná brána*), was built here in 1841 in Empire style. This marked the end of the city's construction of defensive fortifications. Vyšehrad was incorporated into Prague as the sixth city district in 1883, and a national cemetery (Slavín) of honor was laid out atop the cliff. Today, Vyšehrad, with its park-like grounds, is a popular excursion site for the residents of Prague.

### Viewing the *Vyšehrad

It's easy to reach on the subway, which stops at Vyšehrad station. From there, head West past the modern cultural center (which affords a good view) and along the old fortifications to the early Baroque

*Excursions in and around Prague*

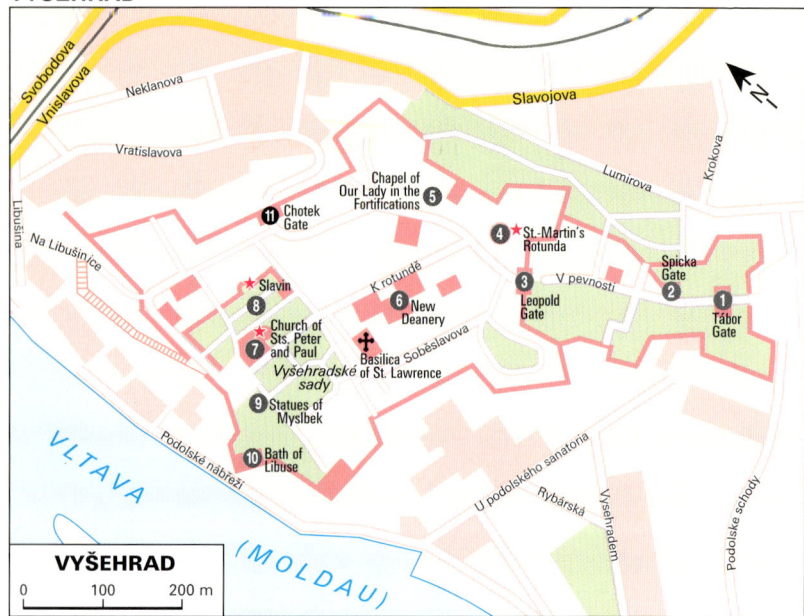

**VYŠEHRAD** *(MOLDAU)*

0    100    200 m

**Tábor Gate ❶** (*Táborská brána*, 1655). This is an outpost of the fortifications which were dismantled in 1866. After passing through the gate, you can see the remains of the late Gothic **main gate ❷** (*Špička brána*) on your right, and the defensive wall erected under Charles IV. The fortress begins at the **Leopold Gate ❸** (*Leopoldova brána*, built in 1678). Beyond that, on the right, is the oldest structure of Vyšehrad, **★St. Martin's Rotunda ❹** (*Rotunda svatého Martina*).

The chapel was built around 1270. It is the only structure still remaining from this era; although the Romanesque chapel did, admittedly, undergo a course of restorations in 1878-89, when a new south portal was added in place of the original west portal.

Close-by is the **Chapel of Our Lady of the Fortifications ❺**. Until 1784, this chapel was a site of pilgrimage; worshipers flocked to see the statue of Our Lady

*Right: Arcades in the Slavín National Cemetery.*

of Loreto. Closed for a hundred years, it was consecrated anew at the end of the 19th century. Southwest of the rotunda is the former **Canons' House ❻** dating from the year 1770; today, it houses an exhibit about the history of Vyšehrad.

West of this is the **★Church of Saint Peter and Saint Paul ❼** (*Kostel svatého Petra a Pavla*). Its tower, overlooking the Vtlava Valley, was not completed until 1902. The Romanesque structure, dating from the time of Vratislav I, was remodeled as a five-aisle basilica under Charles IV. Thereafter, the church underwent three additional remodeling jobs: one in Renaissance style, one in Baroque, and finally, between 1885 and 1887, the final transition into the neo-Gothic edifice you see today, which has become something of a Vyšehrad landmark.

Above the main entrance is a relief of the Last Judgment. In the interior, the first chapel of the southern side aisle has a Romanesque sarcophagus which probably contains the mortal remains of one of the Přemyslid rulers.

*Slavín* 🔘, the cemetery of honor, which is also a national cultural monument, is located north of the church. It is surrounded on three sides by arcades. More than 50 Czechoslovakian artists, scientists and politicians are buried here in one large communal crypt. In the cemetery lie another 500 famous personalities. Among these are composers, Antonín Dvořák and Bedřich Smetana; authors, Jan Neruda, Karel Čapek, and Božena Němcová; poet, Karel Hynek Mácha; violinist, Jan Kubelik; artist, Alfons Mucha; sculptors, Josef Myslbek, Bohumil Kafka and Ladislav Šaloun and many more. Some of the artists mentioned here designed a number of the gravestones, including those marking their own last resting-places. In the North, toward the Vtlava, is a copy of the equestrian statue of St. Wenceslas. The original by J.G. Bendl (1678), first stood on Wenceslas Square. Further to the South is a **group of statues** 🔘 by Myslbek, depicting themes and figures from Bohemian legends, including Libuše and her husband Přemysl as a ploughman.

Remains of a 15th century watchtower on the south side of the fortress wall have been declared as the **Bath of Libuše** 🔘. A more likely explanation is that foodstuffs delivered by ships were hoisted through a crevice in the stone. Before leaving Vyšehrad, take the opportunity to enjoy the lovely view. The panorama encompasses the Vtlava Valley, Hradčany Castle across the river and, to the east, the districts of Nusle and Vinohrady. Exit the castle through the **brick gate** 🔘 on the north side of the grounds. There is a small museum with information about the fortress's history and development.

## ŽIŽKOV
### Main Cemetery and New Jewish Cemetery

In the district of Žižkov, bunches of metal "asparagus spears" seem to thrust

upwards into the sky over Prague. This is the 216-meter-tall television tower (*Televizní vysílač*), built between 1986 and 1991. There is a cafe at 62 meters, and an observation deck at 97 meters.

Prague's **Main Cemetery** (*Olšanské hřbitovy*) and the **New Jewish Cemetery** (*Židovské hřbitovy*) are located further east. Both cemeteries are noteworthy for their gravestones, in neo-Gothic, neo-Renaissance and art nouveau styles, but some of the modern works by famous Czechoslovakian sculptors and architects are also worth viewing. One of the main attractions in the New Jewish Cemetery is the grave of Franz Kafka (1883-1924). The simple gravestone is on the right after you enter the cemetery, in a row near the wall. Many of the inscriptions on the gravestones are in German, testimony to the days when Prague was a city of three cultures. Kafka's sisters are also buried here. A bronze memorial plaque honors Dr. Max Brod (1884-1968), friend and publisher of Kafka's works, who died in Tel Aviv.

*Excursions in and around Prague*

## TROJA CASTLE AND *PRAGUE ZOO

On the northern banks of the Vtlava is the city district of Troja. **Troja Castle** (*Trojský zámek*) is situated on a terraced hill behind a symmetrically-landscaped park. To the East is a large orchard, laid out in a diamond pattern. The palace was built in 1679-80 as the summer residence of Count Wenzel Adalbert von Sternberg, according to plans by the French architect, Mathey. Beyond the stairs, a portal leads into the large and noteworthy Emperor's Hall, transformed into a grand Baroque eulogy to the greatness of the Hapsburg dynasty through the paintings in oil and tempera by the brothers Godin (Godyn) of Antwerp. The frescoes in the other rooms are by the Italian artist Francesco Marchetti who, with the help of his son Giovanni, also decorated the count's chapel.

*Above left: On the Karlštejn Castle bastion.*
*Above right: In the Holy Cross Chapel.*

The **\*Prague Zoo** (*Zoologická zahrada*) next door gained renown by successfully rebreeding the Przewalski wild horses. For an overview of the zoo, take the cable car up a nearby hill, where you can enjoy the panorama, not only of the zoo, but also of Prague and the Vtlava Valley. The zoo is home to more than 2,500 animals of 600 different species. The visitor can stroll through the grounds over a total of 12 kilometers of paths. The zoo is one of the largest in Europe, and, thanks to its location, also one of the loveliest. It can be reached by Vtlava ship from the Palacký Bridge or from the Rudolfinum (mooring at Stromovka).

## EXCURSION TO *KARLŠTEJN CASTLE

The mighty **\*\*Karlštejn fortress**, only 30 kilometers from Prague, is a popular destination for people on day-trips. Emperor Charles IV erected the fortress on a 320-meter-high limestone cliff. French cathedral master builder, Mathieu d'Arras oversaw the Gothic construction. Ever since, the fortress has towered above the wooded heights like a fairy-tale castle in Bohemian Karst. The fortress was designed as a stylish place for the Emperor to relax and a safe place to store Imperial gems, the Imperial crown, precious relics and documents. Seven Houses of Worship and chapels clarified the spiritual power of the regent. The various building sections were carried out on five terraces, according to the hierarchical order, from bottom to top.

From the parking lot, the visitor arrives in a quarter of an hour to the outer fortress, to the Burgrave's Courtyard and then to the actual Castle Courtyard. Little remains of its original splendor, such as the Imperial work-room, with its pari-colored paneling and wooden ceiling. In the nearby **Tower of Our Lady**, the chapter church of the Virgin Mary, there is an apocalypse cycle with the first realistic portraits of Charles IV. Semi-precious stones glitter from the walls of the adjacent Catherine's Chapel, formerly reserved for the emperor alone.

The heart of the castle beats in the Great Tower: the Imperial gems and the Bohemian coronation insignia were once stored in the **Holy Cross Chapel** on the second floor. Today, these are kept in Vienna's Hofburg and in Prague's St. Vitus Cathedral. In the lavishly gilded vaulting shine Viennese glass stars and 4,000 semi-precious stones. In this chapel, Master Theodorich and his assistants painted a cycle of 127 true-to-life panel paintings with saints, angels and prophets, around 1360. Five frescoes are also ascribed to them. Some original portraits are on display in Prague, replaced by copies here. The castle has often changed its appearance, as it did in the 16th century, to a Renaissance style. From 1887 to 1899 pseudo-Gothic renovations took place. Architectural sins prompted the UNESCO to forbid its listing on the World Heritage list.

Accommodation connected by public transportation to the city center. The metro stops at midnight. Check the bus and tram schedule in advance.

## VYŠEHRAD AND SOUTH PRAGUE

**Corinthia Towers**, P-4, Kongresová 1, Tel. 61191111, Fax 61211673. **Corinthia Panorama Hotel** , P-4 (Pankrác), Milevská 7, Tel. 61161111, Fax 426263. **Oáza**, P-4, Jeremenkova 106, Tel. 61215071-4, Fax 61215075. *BOTEL:* **Racek**, P-4, Dvorecká louka, Tel. 61214389, Fax 61214390.

## VINOHRADY, ŽIŽKOV, KARLÍN AND EAST PRAGUE

**Hilton Atrium**, P-8 (Karlín), Pobřežní 1, Tel. 24841111, Fax 24811932. **Don Giovanni**, P-3, Vinohradská 157a, Tel. 67031111, Fax 67036704. **Karl Inn**, P-8 (Karlín), Šaldova 54, Tel. 24811718, Fax 24812681. **Luník-Garni**, P-2, Londýnská 50, Tel. 252701, Fax 256617. **Libeň**, P-8 (Libeň), Zenklova 37/2, Tel. 6834009, Fax 6834014.

## LETNÁ AND THE NORTH SIDE OF PRAGUE

**Praha**, P-6 (Dejvice), Sušická 20, Tel. 24341111, Fax 24311218. **Holiday Inn Praha**, P-6 (Bubeneč), Koulova 15, Tel. 24393111, Fax 2431 0616. **Splendid**, P-7, Ovenecká 33, Tel. 373351-9, Fax 382312. **Kozlovka**, P-6, Kozlovská 24, Tel. 325882, Fax 3113 373. **Orlík**, P-6 (Dejvice), Terronská 6, Tel. 57210410, Fax 57215263.

## SMÍCHOV AND WEST PRAGUE

**Club Hotel Bohemia**, P-6, Ruzyňská 197, Tel. 3162401, Fax 3163442. **Vaníček**, P-5, Na Hřebenkách 60, Tel. 350714, 352890, Fax 350619. **Coubertin**, P-6, Atletická 4, Tel. 352851-3, Fax 20513208. *BOTEL:* **Admirál**, P-5, Hořejší nábřeží, Tel. 57321302, Fax 549616. **Vila Maria**, P-6, Čistovická 37, Tel. /Fax 779200.

## KARLŠTEJN

Train from Prague's Smíchov station. A number of travel agencies in Prague offer bus tours to Karlštejn. Open Jan – March, Nov and Dec 9:00 a.m. – 3:00 p.m., April and Oct 9:00 a.m. – 4:00 p.m., May, June, Sept 9:00 a.m. – 5:00 p.m., July and Aug 9:00 a.m. – 6:00 p.m. Closed for lunch noon to 1:00 p.m. The Holy Cross Chapel has been reopened to the public after more than a decade of renovations ( open only 1.7. – 31.10., groups with a max. of 10 persons). Registration by e-mail: rezervace@pusc.cz In addition, the visitor can see a video of the chapel in the castle shop. There is a wax museum in Karlštejn, U Karla IV Nr. 174. The display provides a brief survey of Czech history, completed by multimedia elements (daily 9:00 a.m. – 6:00 p.m.)

*Excursions in and around Prague*

69

## GALLERIES AND MUSEUMS

Prague is a museum city in two senses. First, in that merely strolling through the city's streets is like leafing through a stone history book. Everywhere you look, your eye alights on ornamental details or architectural artefacts, which are present in a seemingly endless wealth. Prague also has a large number of important museums. In most cases, the larger collections are dispersed among many buildings, often lying in different districts of the city.

### The National Gallery

The **National Gallery** (*Národní galerie*) consists of four institutions with permanent and occasional special exhibitions, as well as three galleries which have temporary exhibitions only. The

*Above: The National Gallery's collection of paintings in the Sternberg Palace. Right: Exhibit in St. George's Monastery.*

permanent collections are in the Sternberg Palace, St. George's Monastery, the St. Agnes Convent and in Zbraslav Castle in the south of Prague.

Indubitably the most international of these is in the **Sternberg Palace**. This Baroque building is tucked away behind the Archbishop's Palace on Castle Square. Focal point of the extensive collection is German medieval and Renaissance painting, 15th- to 17th-century Dutch and Flemish masters, the Italian Renaissance, and French painting of the 19th and 20th centuries. One of the most valuable works in the collection is Albert Dürer's *Rosary Festival*, painted in Venice in 1506. More popular, at least in terms of drawing crowds, is the collection of French painting, notably works by the Impressionists and post-Impressionists. These range from Eugène Delacroix through Gustave Courbet to Manet, Monet, Renoir, van Gogh, Toulouse-Lautrec, Gauguin, Henri Rousseau, all the way up to Georges Braque, as well as Chagall and Utrillo.

*Information page 75*

During the Communist regime, visitors were always amazed at the extent of the museum's remarkable collection of modern art, particularly works by Picasso, which were seldom, if ever, shown in the West. Outsiders tended to forget that Picasso, when in exile, was by no means on good terms with the Franco regime; but rather, as a member of France's Communist Party, was not exactly opposed to the former socialist state. But 20th-century Austrian and German art is also represented with works by Gustav Klimt, Egon Schiele, Oskar Kokoschka and Franz Marc. There are even some sculptures by Rodin, who had many admirers in Prague, not a few of whom attempted to follow in his footsteps.

**St. George's Monastery** is not far from the Sternberg Palace, on the grounds of Prague Castle. If you undertake a visit through the exhibit here, you should come armed with a healthy interest in Christian paintings, from the Gothic age to the Baroque. This former Benedictine monastery houses, among other things,

the world's largest collection of 14th-century panel paintings, mainly works from Bohemia, Germany and Italy. Other works in the gallery range from Rudolphian Mannerism up to Late Baroque. Another branch of the National Gallery located in the Castle, is housed in the former **Riding School**, which presents rotating exhibits of contemporary art.

Down in the city, near the Vtlava and just east of Josefov, is the **St. Agnes Monastery**. The permanent collection here features works by Czech painters and sculptors of the 19th century, including many sculptures by the ubiquitous Josef Václav Myslbek, whose works are scattered throughout the entire city. Fans of figurative painting will enjoy the works by Josef Mánes and Mikoláš Aleš.

The fourth museum of the National Gallery, **Zbraslav Castle** (King's Hall), can be reached by bus 129, 241 or 243 from the main bus depot Smíchov (metro station). The building, with its Baroque

*Galleries and Museums*

elements, is a former Cistercian monastery, which was originally a hunting palace and a chapel. Noteworthy is the depiction of the founding of the monastery by King Václav II, shown in a ceiling fresco by Wenzel Lorenz Reiner in the main hall of the central wing.

Sculptures by Czech masters of the 19th and 20th century are exhibited inside as well as outside in the park. The prolific Josef Václav Myslbek is represented in Zbraslav, as is Ladislav Šaloun, who sculpted the Hus Monument on the Old Town Ring, and Bohumil Kafka, the artist who created the monumental life-like statue of Jan Žižka on Vítkov. Those interested in learning more about the development of sculpture in Bohemia (influenced by such greats as Rodin and Maillol), should have a look at this museum, although it's out of the way in the rather less-than-attractive suburbs.

*Above: In the Great Exhibition Palace. Right: Collection of musical instruments in the National Museum.*

The gallery in the **Riding School** in the Waldstein Palace and the **Kinský Palace** on the Old Town Ring display temporary exhibits. The storerooms of the Kinský Palace seem to contain an inexhaustible supply of drawings and graphics by masters from around the world from over the last five centuries, displayed in rotating exhibitions. Highlights include works by such artists as Dürer, Rembrandt, Goya and Dalí, to name but a few.

The **Great Exhibition Palace** (*Veletržni palác*), on this side of the train underpass in front of the historical old exhibition grounds on Stromovka, has finally been completely restored after its severe fire damage in 1974. This functionalist structure was for a time the world's largest exhibition center after its completion in 1929. It is still impressive with its two spacious, high-ceilinged halls – formerly used mainly to display large machines and industrial objects. Today, modern Czechoslovakian art from 1900 to 1995, 19th and 20th century French art and 20th century European art are displayed here.

### National Museum

Like the architecture of the National Theater, the **National Museum's** (*Národní muzeum*) construction has about it a sense of the nationalistic pathos that prevailed in the late 19th century, turned to stone.

Even before you enter the exhibits, you're greeted by the statues and busts of important historic figures, which line the stairway under the dome. This theme is continued in the Pantheon, a kind of Czech hall of fame spread over two floors. Among all the heroes, only two women are to be found, authors Božena Němcová and Eliška Krásnohorská. All the other pedestals, and there are more than 40 of them, support the figures of men, including the composers Dvořák and Smetana, the great reformer Jan Hus,

the pedagogue Jan Amos Komenský (Comenius) and the first President of the ČSR, Tomáš G. Masaryk. Also on the second floor, you'll find a well-curated exhibit of the pre-history and early history of the territory of the Czech and Slovakian states. Although there is a very general description in English of the individual cultural epochs, the detailed explanations are unfortunately all in Czech language.

Other exhibits in this wing present the history of the currency as well as the more modern history of the Czech people since their sense of national identity began to develop in the 19th century.

The opposite wing houses an extremely detailed collection of mineralogy and petrography. If you've never realized the myriad forms and colors which inanimate nature can present, this exhibit will be truly an eye-opener.

One wing on the second floor has a zoological department; the other, a paleontological one. For lovers of smaller creepy-crawly things, the National Museum has one of the world's largest insect collections. In the basement, as well as a salad bar, there is also space for cultural, historical, or other relevant temporary exhibits.

Like the National Gallery, the National Museum also has branches throughout the city displaying parts of its collection. Music lovers are in for a special treat, for there are three museums in this category. The **Villa America** is dedicated to the works of Dvořák, the **Villa Bertramka**, those of Mozart, and the former **Waterworks** displays an exhibit on the works of Smetana.

The **Lapidarium** on the Exhibition Grounds (*Výstaviště*) houses a noteworthy exhibit of building fragments from historic houses which have been razed. History buffs will want to visit the **Lobkovicz Palace** when they're touring Prague Castle. In addition to the permanent exhibit documenting the most important epochs of Bohemian history, the building is also a venue for special exhibitions and concerts.

**Other Museums**

The extensive, world-wide unique collection in the **★★Jewish Museum** (*Židovské muzeum*) is distributed throughout many buildings in the Josefov. The Pinkas, Maisl, Klausen and Spanish Synagogues are all part of the museum, as is the Old Jewish Cemetery. Paradoxically, it was the Nazis who laid the cornerstone for this collection: they gathered valuable religious artefacts from exterminated communities, which were to be presented in a "Museum of an Extinct Race" following the "final victory."

If you'd like to learn something about the city itself, stop in at the **Museum of the Capital City of Prague**, located north of the Florenc bus depot. The incredibly detailed model of the city depicts, for example, the layout of Josefov at the turn of the century, before its so-called *Assanierung* (the Austrian term for

*Above: A small marionette museum in Charles Lane.*

building improvements for reasons of hygiene or society). Here, too, is the original face of the large clock of the Old Town Hall, designed by Josef Mánes.

The **Museum of Decorative Arts** (*Umělecko průmyslové muzeum*) is located between the Rudolfinum and the Old Jewish Cemetery. Fans of antique furnishings will particularly enjoy this museum. In addition to lovely pieces of furniture, with exquisite stone and wood inlays, the museum also houses delicate double-walled glass containers with gold and silver foil between the layers, Meissen porcelain and majolica. There are descriptions of the exhibits in several languages. Hall IV offers a good view of the Old Jewish Cemetery. The museum also has a small cafe.

The Kaunitz Palace (*Kaunický palác*) in Prague's center is devoted to the works of the most famous Czechoslovakian art nouveau artist, Alfons Mucha (1860-1939). The **Alfons Mucha Museum** displays many lithographs, paintings and drawings on permanent loan from the Mucha Foundation. The visitor gains a comprehensive glimpse into the world of this artist made famous through his billboard designs for the fin-de-siècle theater legend, Sarah Bernhardt.

As other big cities, Prague also has its **Wax Museum**. It is located near Wenceslas Square. There are replicas of politicians and artists, among them Václav Havel, Václav Klaus and Karel Gott.

The **Prague Police Museum** in the southern part of the New Town, near the Villa America, is even more realistic than its American counterpart, the Chicago Police Museum. It displays the reality of a police officer's work. Particularly spectacular cases of criminal activity are documented here in interesting detail. To calm the fears of the timid, the police have already roped off and inspected the museum's chaotic and very realistic scene of the crime, and outlined the position of the corpse in chalk.

## GALLERIES AND MUSEUMS

## MUSEUMS IN PRAGUE

🏛 *NATIONAL GALLERY (Národní galérie)*: open Tues-Sun 10:00 a.m. – 6:00 p.m.
**Sternberk Palace** (*Šternberský palác*), P-1, Hradčanské nám. 15, Tel. 20314599.
**St. George's Monastery** (*Klášter svatého Jiří*), P-1, Prague Castle, Jiřské nám. 33, Tel. 87320536.
**St. Agnes Monastery** (*Anežsky klášter*), P-1, U Milosrdných 17, Tel. 24810628.
**Zbraslav Castle** (*Zámek Zbraslav*), P-5, Zbraslav; Tel. 57921638-9.
**Riding Hall of the Prague Castle** (*Jízdárna Pražského hradu*), P-1, U Prašného mostu 55, Tel. 24373232.
**Wallenstein Riding School** (*Jízdárna Valdštejnského paláce*), P-1, Valdštejnská 2, Tel. 536814.
**Exhibition Palace** (*Veletržní palác*; modern and contemporary art), P-7, Dukelských hrdinuš 47.
🏛 *NATIONAL MUSEUM (Národní muzeum)*:
**National Museum**, P-1, Václavské nám. 68, Tel. 24497111, Mon-Sun 9:00 a.m. – 6:00 p.m., Oct-Apr to 5:00 p.m., closed first Tuesday of the month.
**Lapidarium** P-7, Výstaviště, Pavillon 422, Tues-Fri 10:00 a.m. – 6:00 p.m., Sat, Sun 12:00 noon – 6:00 p.m.
**Lobkowicz Palace**, P-1, Jiřská 3 (Castle), Tel. 537306, Tues-Sun 9:00 a.m. - 5:00 p.m..
**Museum of Czech Music / Dvořák-Museum**, P-2, Ke Karlovu 20, Tel. 298214, Tues-Sun 10:00 a.m.– 5:00 p.m.
**Smetana Museum**, P-1, Novotného lávka 1, Tel. 24229075, Mon, Wed-Sun 10:00 a.m. – 5:00 p.m.
**Villa Bertramka** (**Mozart Museum**), P-5, Mozartova 169, Tel. 543893, Apr-Oct Mon-Sun 9:30 a.m. – 6:00 p.m., other months to 5:00 p.m.
🏛 *JEWISH MUSEUM (Židovské muzeum)*:
**Pinkas Synagogue**, Široká ul., **Maisl Synagogue**, Maislova 10, **Klaus Synagogue**, U starého hřbitova 4, **Spanish Synagogue**, Vězeňská 1, the **Old Jewish Cemetery**, Široká ul., and **Ceremonial Hall** are part of the **Jewish Museum**, (www.jewishmuseum.cz) Entrance tickets: U starého hřbitova 3a, Tel. 2317191. Tickets are valid for all sights belonging to the Jewish Museum. **Old-New Synagogue**, Červená ul.; a separate entrance fee is levied. The sights in Josefov are open April-October from 9:00 a.m. to 6:00 p.m. and November-March from 9:00 a.m. to 4:30 p.m., daily except Saturdays and Jewish holidays.
🏛 *OTHER MUSEUMS:*
**Museum of the City of Prague** (*Muzeum zhlavního města Prahy*), P-8, Na Poříčí 52, Tel. 24816772, Tues-Sun 9:00 a.m. – 6:00 p.m. **Museum of Applied Arts** (*Uměleckoprůmyslové muzeum*), P-1, 17. listopadu 2, Tel. 24811241, Tues-Sun 10:00 a.m. – 6:00 p.m.

**National Technical Museum** (*Národní technické muzeum*), P-7, Kostelní 42, Tel. 3736519, Tues-Sun 9:00 a.m. – 5:00 p.m.
**Vyšehrad** (national monument), P-2, Soběslavova 1, Tel. 39665132, Apr-Oct daily 9:30 a.m. – 5:30 p.m., other months to 4:30 p.m.
**Strahov Monastery** (*Strahovský klášter*), P-1, Strahovské dvůr 1, Tel. 24510355, treasures from the Gothic to the Romantic periods, Tues-Sun 9:00 a.m. – 12:00 noon and 1:00 – 5:00 p.m. Includes the **Museum of Czech Literature** (*Muzeum české literatury*), Tues-Sun 9:00 a.m. – 5:00 p.m.
**House of the Black Madonna** (*Dům U Černé Matky boží*), P-1, Celetná 34, Tel. 2421 1732, Czech Cubism, Tues-Sun 10:00 a.m. – 6:00 p.m.
**Náprstek Museum** (Indian Culture), P-1, Betlémské nám. 1, Tues-Sun 9:00 a.m. – 12:00 noon and 12:45 – 5:30 p.m.
**Wax Museum** (*Muzeum voskových figurín*), P-1, Října 13, Mon-Sun 9:00 a.m. – 8:00 p.m.
**Franz Kafka Museum** (*Muzeum Franze Kafke*), P-1, U radnice 5, Tues-Fri 10:00 a.m. – 6:00 p.m., Sat 10:00 a.m. – 5:00 p.m.
**Alfons Mucha Museum** (*Muzeum Alfonse Muchy*), P-1, Panská 7, daily 10:00 a.m. – 6:00 p.m.
**Toy Museum** (*Muzeum hraček*), P-1, Jiřská 6 (Castle), daily 9:30 a.m. – 5:30 p.m.
**Police Museum** (*Muzeum Policie*), P-2, Ke Karlovu 1, daily except Monday 10:00 a.m. – 5:00 p.m.
**Diltrich Pharmacy Museum**, exhibition of antique pharmacy shops (*Expozice historických lékáren*), P-1, Nerudova 32, Apr-Sep Tues-Fri 12:00 noon – 6:00 p.m., Sat, Sun 11:00 a.m. – 6:00 p.m., Oct-Mar Tues-Fri 11:00 a.m. – 5:00 p.m., Sat, Sun 10:00 a.m. – 5:00 p.m. **Glass Museum** (*Muzeum českého skla*), P-1, Staroměstské nám. 26, daily 10:00 a.m. – 8:00 p.m., Nov-Mar to 7:00 p.m. **Museum of Military History** (*Vojenské historické muzeum*; Schwarzenberg Palace), P-1, Hradčanské nám. 2, currently under restoration.
**Puppet Museum** (*Muzeum loutkářské kultury*), P-1, Karlova 12, Apr-Sep 10:00 a.m. – 8:00 p.m., Oct-Mar 12:00 – 6:00 p.m. **Agricultural Museum** (*Národní zemědělské muzeum*), P-7, Kostelní 44, Tues-Sun 9:00 – 11:30 a.m. and 12:30 – 5:00 p.m.
🏛 *ART GALLERIES OF THE CITY OF PRAGUE*: Tues-Sun 10:00 a.m. – 6:00 p.m.
**Old Town Hall**, P-1, Staroměstské nám. 1, Mon-Sun 11:00 a.m. – 5:00 p.m. **House at Stone Bell** (*Dům U kamenného zvonu*), P-1, Staroměstské nám. 13.
**Municipal Library**, P-1, Mariánské nám. 1. Changing exhibitions. **Troja Castle**, P-7, Troja, Tel. 6890761 (19th century Czech painting), Tues-Sun 10:00 a.m. – 6:00 p.m., Nov-Mar only Sat, Sun 10:00 a.m. – 5:00 p.m.

*Galleries and Museums*

75

## EATING OUT

Over 2000 restaurants, inns and beer parlors invite the visitor to eat and drink in the Czech Republic's capital. Gourmets can enjoy Bohemian-Moravian, international and Eastern European cuisine. In the top restaurants, prices are similar to those of other European metropolises.

MacDonald's and other representatives of the fast food cult can be found on the main squares and shopping boulevards. The Royal Mile has, sadly, received the moniker of "Fast Food Lane."

The gastronomy of the city on the Vtlava ranges from the best to the worst of the metier. Refined dining is expensive, but expensive dining is not always refined. Quite inexpensive meals can also be quite excellent.

Tourist traps lurk everywhere. Thus, foreigners are made to pay for extras on

*Above: A Prague tradition – The Chalice Inn (U Kalicha), scene of the novel "The Good Soldier Švejk."*

the bill, which would never be required of their Czech table neighbors: for napkins or spice mixtures as examples.

Often, guests are lured with live music, for which they are made to pay later. It is best to inquire in advance, for should you decide to leave on account of all the extras for music, place settings, etc., then the staff might suddenly say: for you, today is free.

Incidentally, you might experience this sort of scam even at the Café Europa on Wenceslas Square.

It should be a matter of course always to examine the bill. This is especially true of "manually calculated" bills, for all too often there is a miscalculation to the disadvantage of the patron.

### Just like Mother Used to Make

Those who enjoy local and inexpensive cuisine must often put up with smoky inns. In the center, crowded with tourists, *hostinec* (inns) and *pivnice* (beer parlors) are rare. They can be found in side streets or in the local residential areas, such as those found in the Holešovice neighborhood.

If the visitor is prepared to give up a bit of atmosphere, then he will be served roast pork with cabbage and dumplings or sauerbraten with a cream sauce, just like *Maminka* (Mother) used to make.

Often, a main course will cost only between US $ 1.50 and $ 2.00, and $ 0.50 for half a liter of draft beer. Salad bars and vegetarian restaurants abound in the city's center, where one can load up on healthful, vitamin-rich food.

### Life's Elixir Beer

The Czech word for beer (*pivo*) is derived from the the the verb to drink (*pít*). This clearly demonstrates why beer is the greatest thirst-quencher in the land. Those who complain about the food in Prague may at times be justified, but would be incorrect from a local political point of view. For the inhabitants of Prague, an inn is not visited on account of its food but for its beer.

When private property was returned at the beginning of the 1990's, an imminent collapse of the inns threatened. This was particularly true of the **The Cat's Inn** (*U kocoura*). Citizens banded together to salvage the popular inn. They say the best pilsener in the city is still drawn here.

Ever since 1459, the dark 13%-alchohol-content beer with a hint of caramel after-taste has enjoyed great popularity. It is produced in **U Fleků** and only sold here. The price for a half-liter of beer and the hearty cuisine served here has almost reached European levels.

In addition, the beer-drinking foreign contingent is often served becherovka (herbal schnaps) at cut-throat prices. The only way to protect oneself is a with a firm "ne."

And yet, the *U Fleků* is an experience. 450 patrons can fit into the romantic neo-Gothic hall; an additional 500 can fit into the summer garden. The further one goes from the city center, the less the beer costs. Whereas in city-center bars a quarter liter of pilsener can cost up to 80 Krone, a half liter can be had for 15 Krone.

### Unknown noble spirits

Contrary to the ubiquitous beer drunk with food, wine is only partaken of on special occasions. In many restaurants, wines from South Moravia and North Bohemia are offered.

In the better type of inn, imported wines are also decanted, but they are expensive. Famous local vines thrive around Hodonín, Mikulov, Valtice and Znojmo as well as in the North Bohemian Valley of the Elbe.

Archived wines can be recommended, for they mature at least three years, two of these in barrels. But the inexpensive house wines often mature well. Following the grape harvest, *burčák* is served in Prague, comparable to an Austrian *Federweißer*. It tastes like a sweet grape must and quickly brings one to a state of tipsiness.

### Coffee Houses

Little remains of the famed Prague coffee house culture, which left Vienna and Budapest in the dust until the 1940's. But just the remaining bastions of the k.u.k (King and Emperor) monarchy are an experience and a sight worth seeing. During Socialist times, some of the cafes were legendary meeting points for dissidents.

**The Golden Snake** (*U zlatého hada*) is the name of a restaurant on Charles Lane. It used to be Prague's oldest coffee house. Although the atmosphere has changed considerably, good coffee is still served.

The famous **Café Europa** in the hotel of the same name on Wenceslas Square impresses with its two-story art nouveau

*Eating Out*

architecture; strains of coffee house melodies emerge from the piano in the afternoons.

Next door, polished art nouveau lustre is offered by the Café Nouveau in the Representative House as well as by the **Café in the Hotel Paris**.

In the **Savoy**, patrons can enjoy the splendid neo-Renaissance ceilings above their heads while sipping a Viennese coffee. An opulently-gilded coffee house charms its patrons in the **Grand Hotel Bohemia** (Královodvorská 4).

The **Slavia** on the corner of National Boulevard (*Národní třída*) / Vtlava Quay was sold to an American after the opening to the West. Following the sale of this world-famous cafe, nothing much happened for some time. A letter from President Václav Havel to the owners, in which he called for the matter to be reopened, grew into a state affair. In 1997 the *Slavia* was formally opened anew. Even Western news agencies thought the event worthy of mention. The cafe has counted among its guests Hillary Clinton, who sat here with Václav Havel.

The **Café Louvre** celebrated its rebirth under a new name. Around 1900, it was populated by intellectuals, among them Max Brod and Franz Kafka. Today the cafe is known as **Gany's**. Nostalgic advertising posters dominate one of the dining rooms.

The former k.u.k. **Café Radetzky** is also known under the name of **Lesser Town Café** (*Malostranská kavárna*). Kafka is said to have dropped in here following his walks.

Those seeking a modern coffee house culture will find it in the numerous cafe cellars, such as in the **Café Velryba** at Opatovická 24. One sits in a haze of cigarette smoke and talks of cabbages and kings. Among the cafe's guests are Prague's authors and reporters. Less smoky is the trendy cafe **Hogo Fogo** north of the Old Town Ring.

*Above: Ladies' coffee circle in a cafe in the Representative House.*

## RESTAURANTS, WINE BARS

📧 Reservations are recommended, especially on the weekends and holidays, and during vacation times.

### LESSER TOWN AND HRADSCHIN

❌ *EXPENSIVE:* **U Malířů**, Maltézské nám. 11, Tel. 57320000, fine French cuisine and French wines in a medieval ambience. **U Mecenáše**, Malostranské nám. 10, Tel. 533881, Bohemian and international cuisine, 400-year-old wine bar with a celebrity clientele. **U Zlaté hrušky**, Nový Svět 3, Tel. 20514536, Bohemian and international cuisine, game specialties.
*MODERATE:* **Nebozízek**, Petřínské sady 411, Tel. 537905, old Bohemian cuisine including game, Renaissance palace on the Petřín Hill, beautiful view, reached by funicular. **Italia**, Nerudova 17, Tel. 530386, basic, filling Italian cooking, good coffee, cozy atmosphere. **Pallfy Palác Club**, Valdštejnská 14, Tel. 57320570, international cuisine, candlelight ambience.
*INEXPENSIVE:* **U Mikuláše**, Tržiště 5, Tel. 532181, Bohemian cuisine, tranquil atmosphere. **U Vladaře**, Maltézské nám. 10, Tel. 5753 4121, Bohemian / international cuisine, Moravian wine, restaurant, wine bar, club.

### OLD TOWN AND JOSEFOV

❌ *EXPENSIVE:* **Bellevue**, Smetanovo nábřeží 18, Tel. 22220465, wonderful view of the Vltava river and the Castle. **Restaurant in the Municipal House** (**Obecní dům**), nám. Republiky 5, Tel. 22002770, www.obecnidum.cz, considered to be the most beautiful Art Nouveau restaurant in Europe.
*MODERATE:* **Pilsner Restaurant in the Municipal House** (**Obecní dům**), nám. Republiky 5, Tel. 2200 2780, Bohemian cuisine, Pilsner Urquell. **Reykjavík**, Karlova 20, Tel. 22221218, excellent fish entrees. **Mucha**, Melantrichová 5, Tel. 263586, new restaurant in Art Nouveau style, Bohemian cuisine.
*INEXPENSIVE:* **Amadé**, U Milosrdných 10, Tel. 2320101, best Bohemian homestyle cooking at reasonable prices.

### NEW TOWN

❌ *EXPENSIVE:* **Casablanca**, Na příkopě 10, Tel. 2424 0519, Moroccan cuisine, French wines.
*MODERATE:* **Monastery Wine Bar** (**Klášterní vinárna**), Národní 8, Tel. 290596, steaks, Moravian wine. **Pezinok**, Purkyňova 4, Tel. 291996, Slovak specialties.
**Novoměstský Pivovar**, Vodičkova 20, Tel. 22232448, Bohemian dishes.
**Russkij Samovar**, Dittrichova 25, Tel. 299011, www.samovar.cz, best Russian eatery in the country.

## BEER HALLS / PUBS

🍺 **U Fleků**, P-1, Křemencova 11, Tel. 24915118, dark beer from their own brewery, large beer garden. **U Kocoura**, P-1, Nerudova 2, Tel. 538962, Pilsner Urquell beer served here. **U zlatého tygra**, P-1, Husova 17, Tel. 24229020, 13$^{th}$ century cellar, Pilsner Urquell. **U Kalicha**, P-2, Na Bojišti 12, Tel. 290701, Schwejk memorial pub, Radegast beer. **U Glaubiců**, P-1, Malostranské nám. 4, Tel. 57318017, Großpopowitz Ziegenbock (dark beer). **U svatého Tomáše**, P-1, Letenská 12, Tel. 536776, Braník beer. **U dvou koček**, P-1, Uhelný trh 10, Tel. 24229982, Pilsner Urquell. **U Medvídků**, P-1, Na Perštýně 7, Tel. 24211916, summer garden, Budweiser. **Krušovická pivnice**, P-1, Široká 20, Tel. 2316689, Krušovice beer, for night owls.

## COFFEE HOUSES

*COFFEE HOUSES IN THE STYLE OF 1900:* **Kavárna Obecní dům**, P-1, nám. Republiky 5, Tel. 22022763. **Hotel Evropa Café**, P-1, Václavské nám. 25, Tel. 24228117. **Café in the Hotel Paříž**, P-1, U Obecního domu 1, Tel. 24222151. **Savoy**, P-5, Vítězná 5, Tel. 535000. **Café Rudolfinum**, P-1, Alšovo nábřeží 12, very chic, open only until 8:00 p.m.
*OTHER COFFEE HOUSES:* **Café Slavia**, P-1, Národní třída 2, Tel. 24220975. **Malá Strana Coffee House** (**Malostranská kavárna**), P-1, Malostranské nám., Tel. 533092, in a rococo-style house. **Kavárna Velryba**, P-1, Opatovická 24, Tel. 24912484. **Reno Espresso** (in the Museum of Applied Arts), P-1, 17. listopadu 2, Tel. 2481 1307. **Dolce Vita**, P-1, Široká 15, Tel. 2329192, good Italian coffee. **The Globe**, P-7, Jankovského 14, Tel. 66712610, e-mail: theglobe@ecn.gn.apc.org. Cafe with bookshop, has a large American clientele.
*CAFES:* **Café Poet**, P-1, Zahrada na Baště, Tel. 2051 5462, quiet, somewhat hidden in the northwest section of the Prague Castle. **Café Ledebour**, P-1, Valdštejnské nám. 3, Tel. 57010412.
**Kavárna u Týna**, P-1, Staroměstské nám. 15, Tel. 2310525, touristy. **Cybeteria-Internet Café**, P-1, Štěpánská 18, Tel. 22230707, e-mail: info@cybeteria.cz
**Hogo Fogo**, P-1, Salvátorska 4, Tel. 2317023.
**Bohemia Bagel & Internet Café**, P-1, Újezd 16, Tel. 530921, and Masná 2, Tel. 24812560, bagels, sandwiches, Internet terminals, www.bohemiabagels.cz

## TEA ROOMS

**Dobrá čajovna**, P-1, Václavské nám. 14, Tel. 2423 1480. **Růžová čajovna**, P-1, Růžová 8, Tel. 262791.

*Eating Out*

## PRAGUE'S NIGHT-LIFE

### Theater

A first-time visitor to Prague could well gain the impression that the Golden City is one giant theater. The buildings, the river and the bridge form the best stage backdrop that one could hope for.

Famous and time-honored is the **National Theater**, which has classical dramas in the repertory as well as grand opera (usually with introductions in German and English). If you prefer to see staging that is true to the composer's wishes, rather than the kind of interpretative readings one often encounters in Europe – until now, at any rate – you have come to the right place. The same is true of the **State Opera** in the Smetana Theater. Here, too, the architecture emphasizes the character of the classical productions. Recently, however, this theater has seen some daring productions involving new, international performers.

A truly historic site is the **Estates Theater** (*Stavovské divadlo*) between Na příkopě and the Old Town Ring, called the Tyl Theater in reference to a period following the Second World War. Here, in 1786, Mozart's *The Marriage of Figaro* made such waves that the composer was able to report to Vienna that *Figaro* was all you could hear in the city. He was subsequently commissioned to compose an opera for the Estates Theater and returned to the site of his greatest success with *Don Giovanni*. In October, 1787, he conducted the world premiere, thereby bringing the Estates Theater into the annals of history. Even today, Mozart performances are among the highlights in this neo-classical theater. If you aren't bothered by the interference of synchronization, you can listen to performances with headphones, in English.

*Right: A street theater's Death Dance Sequence.*

Mozart operas are also the core of the repertoire of the **National Marionette Theater** (*Národni divadlo marionet*) in the *Žatecká*. The music is recorded; the clever, attractive puppet staging is calculated to win smiles from its audience. Perhaps the most famous of Prague's marionette theaters is, however, the **Divadlo Špejbla a Hurvínka**. For decades, the expressive puppets here have been presenting light pieces dealing with the ever-popular subject of father-son relations.

Light, amusing entertainment can also be found at the **Karlín Music Theater** (*Hudebni divadlo*), an art nouveau building on the edge of the city between the New Town and Karlín, which specializes in operetta and musicals. Among the best theaters presenting works almost exclusively in Czech, are the **Divadlo Na Vinohradech**, the **Studio Ypsilon** and the **Divadlo Za branou II**. It may be worth the effort to try to go to a play here, provided you already know the piece.

Pantomime can be found in the **Divadlo Na zábradlí** and the excellent **Branické divadlo pantomímy**; the former also presents regular plays. Director here is Ladislav Fialka, whose brand of pantomime has now become a classic, placing him alongside Marcel Marceau and Samy Molcho in the ranks of the greatest performers of wordless drama.

### Movie Theaters

Prague's cinemas present international films in the original language with Czech subtitles, soon after their release in their home country. To be recommended for their ambiance are the older cinemas in the arcades around Wenceslas Square, especially the **Lucerna.**

### Concerts

Prague is a veritable El Dorado for classical music enthusiasts. There are performances nearly every day in many

of the city's old palaces, historic buildings, and churches. A highlight of the annual calendar is the festival called **Prague Spring**, with numerous events throughout the entire city. The city's best musical institution is the Czech Philharmonic, which regularly enthuses audiences in **Dvořák Hall** in the Rudolfinum on Jan Palach Square. The building itself is an impressive neo-Renaissance edifice which is also a venue for art exhibitions. An equally impressive space is **Smetana Hall** in the Municipal Building on Republic Square. Fabulous for its architecture and majestic acoustics, and for the level of musical offerings, is **St. Vitus Cathedral**, especially when the tones of organ and full chorus boom out and resound through the nave. In season, there are several concerts a week in the **Clementinum**, often twice a day.

Prague is also famous for its lively **Jazz scene,** and Czechoslovakian musicians are among the best in the world. The most famous Prague jazz club (and the oldest in Europe) is the **Reduta**, founded in 1958. Bill Clinton and Václav Havel performed together here. Every October, Prague hosts an international jazz festival.

### Night-life

In Socialist Prague, the sidewalks were rolled up by 11:00 p.m. at the latest. For those with Western currency, the **Alhambra** on Wenceslas Square, still extant, smacked a bit of a provincial Moulin Rouge or some other (dis)reputable night spot with a reputation for slightly shady adventures. In the field of nightclubs, not much has happened, quantitatively or qualitatively, of late; but the disco field has seen considerable activity. Around Wenceslas Square, there have always been a whole row of expensive dance spots, usually inundated with the combined forces of high school classes visiting from the West. **Carioca**, with its open-air balcony, broadcasts its music throughout the lower part of the square, and is known today as the hit of the

Night-Life

*Above: Concert in the Rock Café.*

Golden Cross. Similar to the Wenceslas Square discos in terms of its public, is the open-air disco of the **Lávka Bar** on Charles Bridge. On warm summer nights, the very young and the no-longer-so-young from the West can be found rocking on a small terrace in the shadow of the bridge. The music is dominated by oldie titles. Things are less romantic in the **Rock Café** on Národní třída. Ear-splitting live music deafens the ears of a public comprised, again, predominately of tipsy high-schoolers. After midnight, disco music takes over. A comparable establishment is the well-known **Bunkr**, set up in a former atomic shelter on Lodecká. Some of the best bands in Prague, or, indeed, in the entire world, uphold the reputation of this bar, which is known today as one of the best clubs in Europe. The dance floor of the club **Borát**, on Újezd Street in the Lesser Town, is notable for its extreme smallness. This joint still draws a local crowd, whose hearts – as well as outfits and hairdos – are still in the 1960s and 70s. Further south toward Smíchov on Zborovská, **Futurum** has taken over the building of a former movie theater. Only a few tourists find their way here. When no band is playing, a kind of elegiac air seems to prevail in the emptyish rooms. In the Lesser Town, directly on the Lesser Town Ring, a club which is extremely reasonable and actually meets people's expectations, both in its prices and in what it offers, has established itself on the upper story of a building that used to be the Town Hall for the neighborhood: **Malostranská beseda**. In addition to jazz, a lot of rock music is performed here by local bands.

A special kind of Western enclave appears in the form of **Radost F/X**. This is a gathering-place for chic locals who want to treat themselves to a taste of America, as well as for a portion of the Americans who find Prague so chic that they've decided to settle down for a while. There is a vegetarian restaurant on the upper floor.

One of the loveliest places to go is the **Repre Klub** underneath the Café Nouveau in the Municipal, or Representative, Building. Here, the club's art nouveau rooms house several young rock bands of varying levels of ability, who literally shake the foundations of this venerable old building nearly every evening. In the same building, on the corner, the bar **Formanka,** has a setting reminiscent of the Berlin bar scene in the early 1970s. In the crowded space, its air foggy with cigarette smoke, people philosophize and drink in ample measure. In the window, a plaster bust of Lenin stoically endures the cigarette butt that someone has forced into his mouth.

Things have been looking up for the gay scene since the founding of the "November." An umbrella organization of homosexual citizens, SOHO, publishes *SOHO Magazine* with listings of events, clubs, and meeting-places.

# NIGHT-LIFE

## ADVANCE TICKET SALES OUTLETS

🎫 **Ticketpro**, Salvátorská 10, Tel. 84011150, Fax 24814021, e-mail: orders@ticketpro.cz, *Ticket Sales Outlets:* PIS, Staroměstská radnice, Staroměstské nám. 1, Tel. 24482202; **PIS**, Na Příkopě 20, Tel. 264020; Lucerna, Štěpánská 61, Tel. 24212003. **BTI** (Bohemia Ticket International), Na příkopě 16, Tel. 21612123, 21612124, Fax 21612126. e-mail: btiinter@login.cz, www. ticketsbti.csad.cz

## OPERA AND THEATER

🎭 **National Theater (Národní divadlo)**, P-1, Národní třída 2, Tel. 24913437, www.narodni-divadlo.cz/nd, plays, opera, ballet. **State Opera (Státní opera)**, P-1, Wilsonova 4, Tel. 24227693, 265353, opera, ballet. **Estates Theater (Stavovské divadlo)**, Ovocný trh 1, Tel. 24215001, opera, ballet, plays. **Musical Theater in Karlín (Hudební divadlo v Karlíně)**, P-8, Křižíkova 10, Tel. 21868149, operettas, musicals. **Laterna Magica**, P-1, Národní třída 4, Tel. 24914129, www.laterna.cz, the presentations are a mix of film, theater, dance pantomime, and music, all in one. **Studio Ypsilon**, P-1, Spálená 16, Tel. 292255, plays. **Divadlo Na Vinohradech (Theater in Vinohrady)**, P-2, Náměstí Míru, Tel. 24257604, plays. **Black Light Theater J. Srnec (Černé divadlo J. Srnec)**, P-1, Celetná 17, Tel. 57923397, plays. **Black Light Theater F. Kratochvíl (Černé divadlo F. Kratochvíla)**, P-1, Národní 20, Tel. 24912246, "Anatomy of a Kiss," "Miss Sony." **Spejbl and HurvínekTheater (Divadlo Spejbla a Hurvínka)**, P-6, Dejvická 38, Tel. 3121241, puppet theater for adults and children. **National Marionette Theater (Narodní divadlo marionet)**, P-1, Žatecká 1, Tel. 2322536. **Opera Mozart**, P-1, Novotného lávka 1, Tel. 21082288, modern opera. **Pyramida**, P-7, Výstaviště, Tel. 1041, 24814020, musical "Grease." **Spirála**, P-7, Výstaviště, Tel. 20103380, musical "Evita."

## CONCERT HALLS

🎵 **Dvořák Hall in the Rudolfinum**, P-1, nám. Jana Palacha, Tel. 2489 3352. **Smetana Hall in the Municipal House (Obecní dům)**, P-1, nám. Republiky 5, Tel. 22002121. **House at Stone Bell (Dům u kamenného zvonu)**, P-1, Staroměstské nám. 13, Tel. 24827526. **Lichtenstein Palace**, Malostranské nám. 13, Tel. 530943. **Chapel of Mirrors in the Clementinum (Zrcadlová síň Klementina)**, Marianské nám., Tel. 21663212. **Lobkowicz Palace** (Castle), P-1, Jiřská 3, Tel. 537 306. **Nostitz Palace**, P-1, Maltézské nám. 1,

Tel. 2051 6671. **Villa Bertramka (Mozart Museum)**, P-5, Mozartova 169, Tel. 543893. **Spanish Hall in the Prague Castle (Španělský sál Pražského hradu)**, P-1, Tel. 24373 368. **Mánes Hall in the St. Agnes Monastery**, U Milosrdných 17, Tel. 24810628. **Historical Staircase in the National Museum**, Václavské nám. 68, Tel. 24497111. **Žofín Palace** on the Slavic Island, Slovanský ostrov, Tel. 2491 8134. Chapel of the **Order of the Knights**, Křižovnické nám. *CHURCHES:* **St. Vitus Cathedral, St. Nicholas Church** (Lesser Town Ring / Old Town Ring), St. George's **Basilica, St. Francis Church, St. Martin Church, Bethlehem Chapel, St. Salvator Church, Church of St. James.** *GARDENS:* **Royal Garden Ball Hall** (Prague Castle), **Wallenstein Garden, Gardens at the Pálffy Palace** and **Vrtba Garden**.

## MOVIE THEATERS AND FILM CLUBS

🎬 **Lucerna**, P-1, Vodičkova 36, Tel. 24216972. **Institut Français**, P-1, Štěpánská 35, Tel. 24216630/61, at 6:00 p.m., free entrance. **Dlabačov**, P-6, Bělohorská 24, Tel. 3115328. **Praha**, P-1, Václavské nám. 17, Tel. 262035. **Ponrepo**, P-1, Bartolomějská 11, Tel. 24231846. **Kino Mat**, P-2, Odborů 7, Tel. 24914604. **U Hradeb**, P-1, Mostecká 64.

## CLUBS AND DISCOS

🎶 *NIGHTCLUBS:* **Alhambra**, P-1, Václavské nám. 5, Tel. 24210463. **Black & White**, P-5, Štefánikova 7. **Lucerna Bar**, P-1, Vodičkova 36, Tel. 24217108. *DISCOS:* **U kamenného stolu**, P-1, Staroměstské nám. 17, Tel. 24212026. **Lávka**, P-1, Novotného lávka 1, Tel. 24214797. **Modrá terasa**, P-1, Na Můstku 9, Tel. 24226288. **Arkadia**, P-1, Na Příkopě 22, Tel. 24213091. **Fromin Disco**, Václavské nám. 21, Tel. 24232319. *ROCK AND POP:* **Klub Újezd**, P-1, Újezd 18, Tel. 538362. **Rock Café**, P-1, Národní 20, Tel. 24914416, **Futurum**, P-5, Zborovská 7, Tel. 544475. Malostranská beseda, P-1, Malostranské nám. 21, Tel. 538651 or 539024. **Radost F/X**, P-2, Bělehradská 120, Tel. 254776. **Roxy**, P-1, Dlouhá 33, Tel. 24810951. *JAZZ CLUBS:* **Agharta**, P-1, Krakovská 5, Tel. 2221 1275. **Café de Paris** (Hotel Paříž), P-1, U Obecního domu 1, Tel. 24222151. **Obecní dům-vinárna**, P-1, nám. Republiky 1, Tel. 22002130. **Metropolitan**, P-1, Jungmannova 14, Tel. 24947777. **Reduta**, P-1, Národní 20, Tel. 24912246. *GAY CLUBS:* **Drakes**, P-5, Petřínská 5, Tel. 534909. **David**, P-8 Sokolovská 77, Tel. 2317882. **Maskot**, P-2, Kolínská 11. **Whiskey Club Old England**, P-2, Šafaříkova 6. Men and women.

*Night-Life*

83

## SHOPPING

In Prague and other Czech metropolises, the same varitey of goods can be found as in the West. Many items are quite inexpensive. Prague is the most expensive town in the country. Less expensive are the surrounding areas; however, the choice is frequently not as varied.

The center for shopping enthusiasts is the **Golden Cross**, composed of Wenceslas Square, the trench (*Na příkopě*), No. 28 října and National Boulevard, with its side streets and lanes. This is not only the most comfortable place to shop, it is also the most expensive.

Popular **provisions** are Prague Ham, Olmützer Quargel (small round cheeses) or Znaim pickles. Also great favorites are Karlsbad wafers, Becherovka bitters, beer, Moravian wine, and fruit liquors such as *slivovice* (made from plums) and *borovička* (made from juniper berries).

*Above: Marionettes – a much sought-after Prague memento.*

Lovely souvenirs are Bohemian **glass**, **Porcelain** and **ceramic ware**. In addition to hand-polished crystal and Karlsbad porcelain with Zwiebelmuster (onion pattern) there are also some modern designs. Those seeking something feudal can obtain chandeliers and mirrors in the k.u.k. (King and Emperor) style.

As Bohemia is considered the land of semi-precious stones, there is jewelry in all shapes. In addition to numerous street vendors (especially on the Charles Bridge and on the sidewalks) jewelers around Wenceslas Square offer a wide range of local products.

**Leather clothing** is still inexpensive. Those seeking **shoes** should look first in the many Bat'a shops in the country.

It is not only children who will find the **dolls**, **marionettes** and fanciful **wooden toys** intriguing. The **"Little Mole"** (*krtek*) of the television series and children's books is available as a stuffed animal or hand-held doll.

Before the opening to the West, there was a great supply of foreign **books**. The choice is somewhat reduced now. Antiquarians can still dig up a treasure or two, but at a cost.

The same is true of **antiques**. For those who wish to find a bargain, it is worth making an excursion to the provinces. However, exportation of precious antiques of national interest is forbidden.

**CDs**, which cost up to 50% percent less than in the West, are a great hit. For **musical scores** and **instruments**, the visitor is advised to do some comparison shopping.

Those wishing to buy an instrument will usually encounter local brands only, and will have to be connaisseurs in order to judge the qualities.

Those with more specialized interests should browse around. There are speciality shops with an appealing range of product lines for anglers, riders, hunters, sports enthusiasts, etc.

Philatelists and numistmatists, who have specialized in editions from the ČSR, ČSSR, ČSFR and the Czech Republic will also get a gleam in their eyes upon sighting the displays.

**Body care products**, such as the cremes of the *Astrid* line with vitamins, panthenol, jojoba oil and UV filters are high quality and quite inexpensive.

*Karlovarská kosmetika* (Karlsbad Cosmetics) offers a good inexpensive range of plant-based products, especially foot-care products (*Karlovarská herbie bylinný krém*). Western cosmetic brands are just as expensive in the Czech Republic as at home.

In the border regions and in the large cities many German and Austrian clients take advantage of the inexpensive modern **hairdressing and cosmetic salon** services. Most of the staff speak German at least.

Czechoslovakian **fashion** is oriented toward international trends, but there are still some small stores around in which the visitor can discover some originally designed and tailored items.

## DEPARTMENT STORES / SHOPPING CENTRES

**Kotva**, P-1, nám. Republiky 8, largest department store, good supermarket section. **Tesco**, P-1, Národní třída 26, good selection of clothing. **Nákupní galerie Myslbek**, P-1, Na Příkopě 19, **Palace Koruna**, P-1, corner Václavské nám. / Na Příkopě.

## SHOES

**Bat'a**, P-1, Václavské nám. 6, P-2, Vinohradská 32.

## GLASS AND PORCELAIN

**Bohemia**, P-1, Národní třída 43. **Bohemia Crystal**, P-1, Celetná 5. **Bohemia Moser**, P-1, Na Příkopě 12 and Malé nám. 11. **Crystalex Shop Praha**, P-1, Malé nám. 6. **Jafa**, P-1, Maislova 15. **Karlsbad Porcelain**, P-1, Pařížská 2. **Sklo Bohemia**, P-1, Na Příkopě 17. **Sklo Exclusive**, P-1, Vodičkova 28, in the ABC Passage. **Caesar Crystal**, P-1, Václavské nám. 20.

## JEWELRY

**Chiuri**, P-1, Národní třída 31. **Exclusive**, P-1, Václavské nám. 47. **Granát**, P-1, Václavské nám. 8 and Dlouhá 28. **Luna**, P-1, Maislova 17. **Shana**, P-1, Na Příkopě 31. **Vili**, P-1, Václavské nám. 9 and 33. **Český granát**, P-1, Celetná 4 and Karlova 44. **Detail**, P-1, Haštalská 8 and Melantrichova 11. **Rapa**, P-1, Na Poříčí 13. **Tom-Bohemia**, P-1, Můstek 10 .

## MUSIC

**Amistar**, P-2, Francouzská 26. **House of Musical Instruments** (*Dům hudebních nástrojů*), P-1, Jungmannova nám. 17. **Antikvariát Hudebniny**, P-1, V Kolkovně 6. **Music Goca**, P-1, V Kolkovně 6. **Popron Multimedia Megastore**, Jungmannova 30, newest CDs, including their own productions. **234**, P-2, Bělehradská 234, rock CDs. **Hudební nástroje**, P-1, Náprstkova 10. **Megastore Koruna**, P-1, Václavské nám. 1. **Supraphon**, P-1, Palackého 1, classical CDs, produced in the Czech Republic.

## FOREIGN LANGUAGE BOOKS

**Cizojazyčná literatura**, P-1, Na Příkopě 27. **Kniha**, P-1, Štěpánská 12. **Knihkupectví Franze Kafky**, P-1, Staroměstské nám. 12, **Knihkupectví Kanzelsberger**, P-1, Václavské nám. 42. **Kafkův dům**, P-1, U Radnice 5. **U Černé Matky boží**, P-1, Celetná 34.

## ANTIQUES

**Antikvariát Keřnek**, P-1, Celetná 31. **Athena**, P-1, U starého hřbitova 4. **Filip Jaeger antikva**, P-1, U Prašné brány 2. **Hodinářství**, P-1, Mikulandská 10. **Profoto**, P-1, Pařížská 12, old cameras and original photographs. **Antique Shop**, P-1, Národni třída 21 and Masarykovo nábřeži 36.

## TOYS, DOLLS, ETC.

**Dřevěné hračky**, P-1, Jilská 7. **Ivre Löfelmannová**, P-1, Jakubská 3 and Veleslavínova 3.

*Shopping*

## METRIC CONVERSION

| Metric Unit | US Equivalent |
| --- | --- |
| Meter (m) | 39.37 in. |
| Kilometer (km) | 0.6241 mi. |
| Square Meter (sq m) | 10.76 sq. ft. |
| Hectare (ha) | 2.471 acres |
| Square Kilometer (sq km) | 0.386 sq. mi. |
| Kilogram (kg) | 2.2 lbs. |
| Liter (l) | 1.05 qt. |

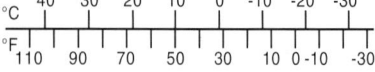

## TRAVEL PREPARATIONS

### Before You Leave
**USA: Czech Tourist Authority**: 1109 Madison Avenue, New York, NY 10028, Tel. (212) 288 0830, Fax (212) 288 0971, e-mail:
**Canada: Czech Tourist Authority**: 401 Bay Street, Suite 1510, Toronto, Ontario M5H 2Y4, Tel. (416) 363 3174, Fax (416) 363 0239.
**United Kingdom: Czech Tourist Authority:** 95 Great Portland Street, London W1N 5RA, Tel. (020) 7291 9925.

The Czech travel agency **Čedok** arranges accommodation and books flight tickets, train reservations, etc.

### Internet sites
*www.czech-tourinfo.cz*
website of the Czech Tourist Authority
*www.pis.cz*
website of the Prague Information Service (PIS) in several languages. Very broad and informative, includes current theater and concert programs.
*www.prag.cz*
sundry information on Prague including accommodations and current weather report.
*www.travel-guide-com/data/cze/*
information on the Czech Republic, including entry and visa requirements, recent exchange rates, important addresses and phone numbers, etc.
*www.timeout.com/prague*
Prague edition of the well-known London city magazine. Much up-to-date information, entertainment and events for the coming week, tips on restaurants, nightlife, accommodations, etc.
*www.muselik.com*
chat forums, classifieds, current exchange rates.

### Climate and Best Travel Times
Prague draws tourists year-round; only in January, February and November do the tourist hordes tend to taper off somewhat. The crowds at the major tourist attractions are at their heaviest during holiday (extended) weekends and during school vacations, including the German and Austrian school breaks.

Prague enjoys a temperate, continental climate with warm, at times humid summers and cold, rather dry winters. The months from April to September promise six to eight hours of sunshine daily.

### Customs Regulations
Articles for personal use may be brought into the country duty-free. Also free from customs and duty charges are: gifts valued no higher than 3000 Kronen (US$ 75), two liters of wine, 1 liter of spirits, 50 g perfume or 250 g eau de toilette and 200 cigarettes or 250 grams tobacco. Foreign currency may be imported and exported in any amount, as may 100,000 (US$ 2,500) Czech crowns (Koruna). The Czech Republic allows the export of all wares for personal use; however, the export of especially valuable antiques is possible only with a special permit. To stimulate enthusiasm for shopping, it even (presumably) refunds to visitors the value-added tax of over 20 %. However, the procedure is complicated, troublesome, and no help to visitors who don't live just over the border: first, on your departure, present the wares to-

gether with the receipt at the Czech customs desk, where the receipt will be stamped. Then, within a half year, return, with the receipt, to the dealer where the wares were purchased; he refunds the tax.

### Entry Regulations

A valid passport is required for visits by citizens of many European countries (UK citizens must have passports); the passport must be valid for a period of three months after date of entry. Visa requirements vary according to country of origin and length of stay: no visa is required for citizens of the USA (visits up to 30 days), Canada (up to 6 months) the UK (180 days) or Japan (3 months); visas are required, however, for citizens of Australia and also "British overseas citizens" when noted in passport. Pets can be brought in only with documentation of rabies immunization. In individual cases, visitors can be required to show sufficient means of support (US $30 per person, per day) as well as evidence of health insurance covering treatment in the Czech Republic. (cf "Medical Care").

### ARRIVAL

### By Air

The international airport Praha-Ruzyně is situated 20 km from, and northwest of, the city center and is managed by Air France. It serves all the large air carriers and has, in addition to a bank with 24-hour currency exchange service, rental car agencies, restaurants, and a post office. Visitors can reach the city center from the airport by taxi, by public bus 119 (change to the Metro line A at Dejvická) or by the airport bus run by the Czech airline ČSA. This bus runs every half hour during peak times, otherwise every hour, to the Republic Square (*nám. Republiky*) in the city center. Tickets are purchased from the driver. The bus makes one stop enroute, at the Metro station Dejvická (Line A).

There are regular flight connectins from Prague to Brno and Ostrava.

**Central Information Service** of the Prague-Ruzyně airport: Tel. 20113314.

**Ticket reservations** for the national carrier ČSA: P-1, V Celnici 5, Tel. 201 04310, www.csa.cz, or in travel agencies.

### By Long-Distance Bus

In addition to organized bus tours, there are long-distance buses that connect Prague with cities in Germany and other countries. The following companies in Prague sell tickets for international routes: Bohemiatour, P-1, Zlatnická 7, Tel. 02/2323877, Fax 2313806; Bohemia Euroexpress International, P-3, Koněvova 126, Tel./Fax 02/22718549, e-mail: doprava@bei.cz; Companies in Germany include: Deutsche Touring, Am Römerhof 17, 60486 Frankfurt/M., Tel. (within Germany) 069/790350 (from outside Germany, replace 069 with 49-69), www.deutsche-touring.com as well as Autobus Oberbayern GmbH, Arnulfstr. 8, 80335 Munich, Tel. 089 (or 49-89) /5490 7560 (connections between Munich and Prague, also between Munich and other Czech cities).

The main terminal for long-distance buses is Florenc, which can be reached by Metro Lines B and C. Buses going to points south and west depart from the Smíchov bus station, which lies on the Metro line B (Anděl station).

### By Car

Drivers entering the Czech Republic (Česká republika, ČR) are required to have a driver's licence, vehicle registration, and the green insurance card. The expressway tax is paid by purchase of a vignette (*dálnicní známky*), available at border crossing points, gas stations, and post offices. In addition to those valid for a year (approximately US $22), vignettes for short visits are now available (one week, approximately US $3.00). Drivers caught without this sticker will be fined.

*Guidelines*

Visiting Prague with an automobile is not recommended. There is a severe shortage of parking in the center; outside of attended parking lots, auto thefts and break-ins are a threat. Prague has one round-the-clock auto repair shop in P-10, Limuzská 12, Tel. 772770 or 0602/315660. All well-known makes of cars can be repaired in Prague.

## By Rail

There are convenient rail connections to Prague from Germany, Austria, Switzerland, Hungary and Poland. Seat reservations on international routes may be required. The "European East" pass is accepted in the Czech Republic. There is also a Czech Flexipass for country-wide travel, and a money-saving 7-day Prague Excursion Pass for travel between any border to Prague and back. Two of Prague's train stations serve international routes: travelers coming from northern and eastern Germany arrive at the Holešovice station (connection to Metro line C). Trains from western and southern Germany, Austria and Switzerland arrive either at Holešovice or at the main railway station (*Hlavní nádraží;* connection to Metro line C).

## PRACTICAL TIPS

### Accommodation

Prague offers hotels, pensions, and rooms in private homes to meet everyone's preference and budget. Breakfast is usually included in the price. Visitors can reserve before the trip, or on arriving in Prague, for example, through Čedok or PIS.

Accommodation is tight during school vacations and long weekends. Local people wishing to rent out rooms in their homes often wait at the train stations for arriving tourists. If you wish to stay in a private home, be sure before accepting the room that the location is convenient by public transportation to the city center.

### Accessibility Issues

Persons with handicapping conditions who need help or information can turn to the Good Will Committee, founded by First Lady Olga Havel (*Výbor dobré vůle*), P-1, Lenovážné nám. 2, Tel. 24216883, to the Czech Association of People with Disabilities, P-8, Karlínské nám. 12, Tel. 248 16997, or to the Union of Disabled Persons, P-1, Konviktská 6, Tel. 24227203.

### Business Hours

Opening hours of shops and other businesses are not regulated by law. Most stores are open Monday through Friday from 7:00 a.m. to 6:00 p.m. and on Saturday from 8:00 a.m. through 12:00 noon. Many supermarkets are open on Sunday as well.

Large department stores have Saturday hours to 4:00 p.m. Many businesses serving the tourist trade stay open until 10:00 p.m. on weekdays. Banks are open Monday through Friday from 8:00 a.m. to 4:00 p.m.

### Currency / Exchange

The unit of currency in the Czech Republic is the Koruna (Kč), or crown, which is divided into 100 Heller. One Koruna is equal to approximately 2 ½ (two and a half) U.S. cents; expect to get roughly forty Koruna for a dollar.

It is strongly recommended to exchange cash and traveler's checks only in banks, or in such outlets as American Express (Václavské nám. 56) and Thomas Cook (Václavské nám. 47). Many other currency exchange outlets (*směnarna*) charge high commissions. If the commission table shows that no commission is charged, the exchange rate offered is probably unfavorable. It is worth while comparing commissions in banks; you should not have to pay more than 2 %, a typical charge among such banks as the *Komerční banka*. The exchange rate offered in hotels is often unfavorable.

Travelers' checks, still the safest way to carry currency, are not accepted like cash in restaurants and shops and must be exchanged beforehand at banks. Credit cards are generally accepted.

### Embassies
**Embassy of the United States of America**, P-1, Tržiště 15, Tel. (2) 5753 0663, Fax 5732 0920.

**Canadian Embassy**, P-6, Mickiewiczová 6, Tel. (2) 7210 1800, Fax (2) 72101890. e-mail: embcanada@chipnet.cz

**British Embassy**, P-1, Thunovská 14, Tel. 5753 0278, Fax 5753 0285. e-mail: info@britain.cz

**Embassy of the Czech Republic in the United States of America**: 3900 Spring of Freedom Street, NW, Washington DC 20008, Tel. (202) 274-9100, Fax (202) 966-8540 or 363-3608 (visa information). e-mail: washington@embassy.mzv.cz

**...in Canada**: 251 Cooper Street, Ottawa, Ontario K2P 0G2, Tel. (613) 562-3875, Fax (613) 562 3878. Email: ottawa@embassy.mzv.cz.

**...in the United Kingdom**: 26-30 Kensington Palace Gardens, London W8 4QY, Tel. (020) 7243 7943, (020) 7243 1115 (visa section), Fax (020) 7727 9654. e-mail: london@embassy.mzv.cz

### Emergencies
**Fire Department**: Tel. 150
**Ambulance**: Tel. 155
**Police**: Tel. 158
**Vehicle Breakdown Assistance**: Tel. 154, 123

### Electricial Current
Electricity in the Czech Republic operates with 220-230 volts AC; continental plugs.

### Events
**January**: Epiphany (Three Kings) parade.

**February**: Mardi Gras (Shrove Tuesday) parades, St. Matthew's parish fair on the Prague exhibition grounds (mid-February to the beginning of April).

**March**: Prague Theater Festival (to October), on the third Saturday. Prague Spring March from the city center to Prčice.

**April**: Beginning of boat rides on the Vtlava River; on April 30 brooms are burned on the Prague Exhibition Grounds to drive out evil spirits, in accordance with an old tradition.

**May**: The International Prague Book Fair takes place during the second week of May in the Palace of Culture. Around the 12th of the month the "Prague Spring" music festival begins, offering performances in many public buildings in the city.

**June**: crew regatta on the Vtlava below the Vyšehrad on the first weekend. Last week of June: international festival of contemporary dance in the National Theater.

**July**: Prague Culture Summer through August.

**August**: Festival of theater and puppet shows on Marksmen's Island (Střelecký ostrov).

**September**: "Prague Autumn" in the Rudolfinum (international festival of classical music), Autumn Fair on the Prague exhibition grounds. A kite-flying competition (Prague-Letná) takes place on the third Sunday. A 10-kilometer race, a tradition since 1887, is held on the last Sunday (Běchovice-Žižkov).

**October**: At the beginning of October, a celebration on the Vtlava marks the end of the water sport season. An international jazz festival takes place in the Lucerna Palace.

**December**: Exhibition of nativity scenes, Christmas markets on the Old Town Ring and in Na přikopě street. On the 26th, the stalwarts go swimming in the ice-cold Vtlava. New Year's Eve is celebrated on the 31st.

*Guidelines*

89

## Lost and Found

Lost (and found) documents should be reported to the police station P-3, Olšanská 3, Tel. 278551-4. Lost property can be sought at: Dopravní podniky office, P-2, Bojišti 5, Tel. 96192173, or P-1, Karolíny Světlé 5, Tel. 24235085.

## Medical Care

Travelers to the Czech Republic are strongly advised to take out a traveler's health insurance policy that will cover them for any medical / hospital treatment needed. In certain cases, proof of such insurance may be demanded at the border or other point of entry. (cf "Entry Requirements"). Medical / dental treatment must be paid for in cash; seek reimbursement (with receipt) from your health insurer. Many doctors speak English. In addition to local hospitals, several foreign clinics serve English speakers: American Medical Center, P-7, Janovského 45, Tel. 80 7756; Canadian Medical Center, P-6, Veleslavinska 30, Tel. 3536 0133; Health Centre Prague, P-1, Vodickova 28, Tel. 2422 0040. The Homolce Hospital, P-5, Roentgenova 2, Tel. 5727 2154 and 5727 2146 has a foreign pavilion.

**After-hours Medical Clinics:** The clinics for adult patients, open from 4:00 p.m. to 7:00 a.m., are located as follows: P-1, Palackého 5, Tel. 24222521; P-2, Sokolská 27, Tel. 299676 and 298116; P-3, Koněvova 205, Tel. 6848685; P-4, Pacovská 31, Tel. 900 57917; P-5, Kartourská 6, Tel. 539269; P-6, Pod Marijánkow 12, Tel. 20513643; P-7, Dukelských hrdinů 1, Tel. 3337 0391; P-8, Mazurská 484, Tel. 8543508; P-9, Lovosická 40, Tel. 86881518; P-10, Nad Olšinami 4, Tel. 7812509.

Pediatric clinics, open from 4:00 p.m. to 7:00 a.m., are located as follows: P-1, Palackého 5, Tel. 24222520; P-2, Sokolská 27, Tel. 299676; P-3, Koněvova 205, Tel. 6847536; P-4, Antala Staška 80, Tel. 421293; P-5, Hostinského 1536, Tel. 597493 and 6522727; P-6, Anastažova 1120, Tel. 20512199; P-7, Dukelských hrdinů 1, Tel. 382326; P-8, Mazurská 484, Tel. 8558292; P-9, Generála Janouška 902, Tel. 81912372, P-10, Vinohradská 159, Tel. 67162573.

**After-hours Dental Clinics**: P-1, Palackého 5, Tel. 24946981 (Mon-Fri 7:00 p.m. to 7:00 a.m., Saturday and Sunday round the clock); P-4, Pacovská 31, Tel. 90057932.

## Newspapers

The English language periodical "Czech Travel News" is available to order by mail from Madi (Husitská 27, 130 00 Prague 3, Fax 004202/6279796).

## Orienting Yourself in the City

Until 1782, the independent little cities that later joined to make up Prague had no system of numbering the houses. One aid to orientation, beginning in the Middle Ages, was the practice of giving a house some sort of name or nickname, made visible through a plaque, for example. Almost two thousand houses in the historic sections of Prague can still be identified this way.

Nowadays, however, the tourist may notice that every house has two numbers: one on a red background and one on a blue background.

The red signs show, together with the letters čp. (*číslo popisné* – so-called conscription number) the consecutive numbering within a historic city: respectively Staré Město (referred to in English as Old Town), Nové Mésto (New Town), Malá Strana (Lesser Town) or Hradčany. This older numbering system was supplemented in 1868 with a new system. What sort of logic were the city fathers of the time employing? The people of Prague revere their Vtlava River; it is their point of reference. The streets running parallel are numbered from South to North. Buildings on the left side of the street have odd numbers; on the right, even numbers. The side streets number their houses as follows: on the left bank, numbers run from East to West; on the right bank, from West to East. Occasionally you will come across the first inscriptions from the end of the 18th century, as the streets were given names in addition to their new system of house numbers. For example, in the Lesser Town, the German street name Welsche Gasse was kept along with its Czech name Vlašská ulice; in the Castle district, you can find the German street name Georgigasse as well as the Czech street name, Jiřská ulice.

### Pharmacies

Pharmacy hours are from 8:00 a.m. – 6:00 p.m. weekdays, Saturday to 12:00 noon. In every section of the city there is at least one pharmacy (*lékárna*) with after-hours service: P-1, Palackého 5, Tel. 24946982; P-2, Belgická 37, Tel. 258189; P-4, Soukalova 33355, Tel. 4014655; P-5, Štefánikova 6, Tel. 57320918; P-8, Hospital Bulovka, Budínova 2, Tel. 83840501; P-10, Šrobárova 50, Tel. 67162694.

### Photography

Film is easily available, western brands are more expensive than at home. Express photo labs develop prints inexpensively.

### Postal System

The post office Hybernská 13 (P-1), Tel. 24225845, is open 24 hours a day for all types of postal services. Telegrams can be sent from any of the 115 post offices in Prague, or by calling the telephone number 0127. **Praha** is the Czech name for Prague. Postage stamps (*známky*) can also be purchased at tobacco kiosks and tobacco shops. Stamps for a postcard cost 7 Kč to points within Europe, or 8 Kč overseas; for letters 8 Kč within Europe, 13 Kč overseas (airmail).

A "post restante" service is offered at the main post office (*Hlavní poštovní úřad*), P-1, Jindřišská 14. Mail can be picked up Mon-Fri between 6:30 a.m. and

8:00 p.m., also on Saturday between 6:30 a.m. and 1:00 p.m. Show your passport as I.D. Holders of American Express cards can also have their mail sent to the American Express office, Václavské náměstí 56 (Wenceslas Square), Tel. 22800249, Fax 22211131. Mail will be held up to one month.

### Public Holidays

Holidays: January 1 (New Years' Day), Easter Monday (varies), May 1 (Labor Day), May 8 (Day of Liberation from Fascism), July 5 (Commemoration of the Slavic Apostles Cyril and Methodius), July 6 (Martyrdom of Jan Hus), October 28 (Founding of Independent Czechoslovakia) and December 24, 25, and 26 (Christmas).

### Public Transportation

cf info box pages 60/61;
metro plan: cf page 59

### Sports

**Bowling**: Corinthia Towers, P-4, Kongresová 1, Tel. 61191326.

**Golf**: Hotel Golf, P-5, Tel. 523251-7, open from the first of April to October 30, daily from 9:00 a.m. to sundown (Standard 72); Praha Karlštejn Golf Club; Strahov Stadium, P-6, Tel. 357803, App. 199 or 7953944.

**Swimming**: Swim Stadium Podolí, P-4, Podolská 74, Tel. 61214343, open Mon-Fri 6:00 a.m. – 10:00 p.m., Sat, Sun 8:00 a.m. – 8:00 p.m., SK Slavia Swim Stadium, P-10, Na Hroudě, Tel. 735552, open Mon-Fri 6:00 – 8:00 a.m. and 6:00 – 8:00 p.m., Sat, Sun 8:00 a.m. – 8:00 p.m.

**Tennis**: Štvanice Stadium in Prague 7, Tel. 2316323 and 2316317.

### Staying Safe

Property crime, including pickpocketing, car theft, etc. has increased in Prague in recent years. Visitors are advised to be careful with briefcases, especially in crowded areas and in public

*Guidelines*

transportation, and not to change money on the street.

Travelers who bring or rent a car should use attended parking lots/garages whenever possible.

### Taxi

Taxi fares are reasonable, as long as the taxi driver is not out to take advantage of tourists.

Either insist that the taximeter is turned on, or negotiate the fare before the ride. If the fare is based on the taximeter, the cheapest tariff 1 is valid for trips within the city (this will be shown on the taximeter on the far right). The tariff is doubled or tripled for late night rides. Arguments over the fare charged can often be settled by demanding a receipt, to which all passengers have a right.

The distance traveled as well as the fare must be noted on the receipt, enabling you to use the receipt if necessary as evidence in a complaint.

The following is just a small selection of taxi companies which accept calls round the clock: AAA, Tel. 1080 and 24322432; BM Taxi, Tel. 8577 and 6897777; Calling, Tel. 7004255; Taxi Arco, Tel. 1088 or 66311254; Radio Taxi Trojická, Tel. 2491 6666; Profi Taxi, Tel. 1035 or 6131 4111; Rony, Tel. 6921958; Sedop, Tel. 67314135 or 67314184; Taxi Praha, Tel. 24916666 or 24911559.

### Telephones

The country code for the Czech Republic, following the international access code, is 420. The area code follows: when calling from outside the country, drop the zero; for Prague, call 420-2.

The international access code for calling out of the Czech Republic is 00; to call numbers in the United States and Canada dial 001 followed by the area code.

International codes are posted in the telephone booths. Telephone cards (*telefonní karta*), available from post of-

fices, are recommended for making long distance calls from phone booths.

Mobile / cell phones on the European standard can be used without difficulty in the Czech Republic.

### Tipping

After a good meal and friendly service, a tip of 5-10% is appropriate.

### Tourist Information

Czech Central for Tourism (*Česká centrálna cestovního ruchu*), Vinohradská 46, 12001 Praha 2, Tel. 02/ 221580411, Fax 24247516, e-mail: visitczech@ccr-cta.cz.

The Prague Information Service (PIS; www.pis.cz) has several branches in the city: Na Příkopé, 20; Staroměstské náměstí 1, Malostranská mostecká věž (open only in summer) and Hlavní nádraží. American Hospitality Center, Na Mustkú 7, Tel. 26 15 74, near Wenceslas Square.

### Weights and Measures

The metric system is used in the Czech Republic. A meter, approximately 39 inches long, is divided into 100 centimeters. Roughly 1.6 kilometers equal a mile. A kilogram (1000 grams) is approximately 2.2 pounds.

### LANGUAGE GUIDE

The Czech language belongs to the Slavic family of languages. Many Czech people speak very good English or German. In any case, knowing several Czech words and phrases makes a polite impression.

### Pronunciation

| | |
|---|---|
| c | . . . . . . . . . . . . . . . . . like tz |
| č | . . . . . . . . . . . . . . . . . like ch |
| d' | . . . . . . . . . . . . . . . . . like j |
| e | . . . . . . . . . . . . . . like short e |
| ě | . . . . . . . . . . . . . . ye as in *yes* |
| h | . . . . . has a strongly breathy sound |

ch . . . . . is a gutteral sound not found in English, is like ch in German *ach*

ň . . . . . . . . . . . like gn in *Cognac*

r . . . . . . . . . . . with rolled tongue

ř . . . . . . . . . . with rolled tongue, followed by s sound as in *measure*

s . . . . . . like unvoiced s in *summer*

š . . . . . . . . . . . . . . like sh

t' . . . . . . . . . not found in English, like t followed by consonant y followed by *ah*: *t'yah*

v . . . . . . . . . like v at the beginning of word/syllable, like f at end

y . . . . . . . . . . . . like short i

z . . . . . . . . . . . . . . . . like z

ž . . . . . . like the s in *measure*

In the Czech language, the stress is always on the first syllable of the word.

All the vowels in Czech are short. If marked with a diacritical (accent) above, or if the u has a tiny circle above it, the vowel sound is drawn out (this does not mean the syllable is stressed!)

### Greetings and Polite Phrases

Hello, good day . . . . . . . *dobrý den*
Good morning . . . . . . . . *dobré jitro*
Good evening . . . . . . . *dobrý večer*
Welcome . . . . . . . *srdečně vítám(e)*
How are you?. . . . . . . *jak se daří?*
Goodbye . . . . . . . . . *na shledanou*
Thank you . . . . . . . . . . . *děkuji*
Please . . . . . . . . . . . . . . *prosím*
Sorry!. . . . . . . . . . . . *odpust'(te)!*
Excuse me! . . . . . . . . . *promiňte!*

### Being Understood

Do you speak English? . . . . . . . . .
*Mluvíte anglicky?*
Do you speak German? . . . . . . . . .
*Mluvíte německy?*
I don't understand . . . . . *nerozumím*
yes . . . . . . . . . . . . . . . . . *ano*
no . . . . . . . . . . . . . . . . . . *ne*
(very) good . . . . . . . *(velmi) dobře*
help! . . . . . . . . . . . . . . *pomoc!*
left . . . . . . . . . . . . . . . *vlevo*
right . . . . . . . . . . . . . . *vpravo*
straight ahead . . . . . . . . . . *rovně*

above . . . . . . . . . . . . . *nahoře*
below . . . . . . . . . . . . . . . *dole*
here . . . . . . . . . . . . . . . . *zde*
there . . . . . . . . . . . . . . . *tam*
who . . . . . . . . . . . . . . . *kdo?*
where? . . . . . . . . . . . . . *kde?*
where to? . . . . . . . . . . . *kam?*
when? . . . . . . . . . . . . . *kdy?*
Where is/where is there...? . . . *Kde je?*
Do you have...?. . . . . . . . *Máte...?*
I need... . . . . . . . . . . *Potřebuji...*
Please give me. . . . . *Dejte mi, prosím*
How much does this cost? . *Co to stojí?*
yesterday . . . . . . . . . . . . *včera*
today . . . . . . . . . . . . . . *dnes*
tomorrow . . . . . . . . . . . . . *zítra*

### Menu (*jídelní lístek*)

mineral water . . . . . . *mineralní voda*
orange juice . . . . *pomerančová št'áva*
coffee. . . . . . . . . . . . . . . *káva*
tea . . . . . . . . . . . . . . . . *čaj*
milk . . . . . . . . . . . . . . . *mléko*
beer . . . . . . . . . . . . . . . . *pivo*
wine (white/red) . . *vino (bílé / červené)*
soup. . . . . . . . . . . . . . . *polévka*
salad . . . . . . . . . . . . . . . *salát*
bread. . . . . . . . . . . . . . . *chléb*
fish (carp / trout) . . *ryba (kapr / pstruh)*
meat . . . . . . . . . . . . . . . *maso*
poultry . . . . . . . . . . . . . *drůbeš*
roast pork . . . . . . . . . . *vepřová*
roast duck . . . . . . . . *kachna pečená*
gulasch . . . . . . . . . . . . . *guláš*
red cabbage . . . . . . . *červené zelí*
sauerkraut . . . . . . . . . . . . . *zelí*
dumpling . . . . . . . . . *knedlíky*
potatoes . . . . . . . . . *brambory*
french fries . . . . *smažené hranolky*
rice . . . . . . . . . . . . . . . *rýže*
pasta. . . . . . . . . . . . . . . *nudle*
dessert . . . . . . . . . . . . . *dezert*
pancake . . . . . . . . . . . *palačinky*
fruit dumpling . . . . . *ovocné knedlíky*
ice cream. . . . . . . . . . . *zmrzlina*

### Numbers (*čisla*)

**0** nula, **1** jeden, jedna, jedno, **2** dva, dvě, **3** tři, **4** čtyři, **5** pět, **6** šest, **7** sedm, **8** osm, **9**

devět, **10** deset, **11** jedenáct, **12** dvanáct, **13** třináct, **14** čtrnáct, **15** patnáct, **16** šestnáct, **17** sedmnáct, **18** osmnáct, **19** devatenáct, **20** dvacet, **21** jedenadvacet, **22** dvaadvacet, **23** třiadvacet, **30** třicet, **40** čtyřicet, **50** padesát, **60** šedesát, **70** sedmdesát, **80** osmdesát, **90** devatdesát, **100** sto, **200** dvě stě, **300** tři sta, **400** čtyři sta, **500** pět set, **600** šest set, **1000** tisíc, **2000** dva tisíce, **5000** pět tisíc, **100 000** sto tisíc, **1 000 000** milión

## AUTHORS

**Bernd F. Gruschwitz** is a historian and Anglicist. He often visited Prague both before and after the fall of the Iron Curtain, and has been following the development of the capital with great interest over the years.

**Hans-Horst Skupy** was born in 1942 in Bratislava, Slovak Republic, but his predilection has always been for Prague.

**Kerstin and André Micklitza**, travel writers of books and articles, specialize in the countries of central eastern Europe. They have thoroughly revised this book and contributed the sections "Presenting Prague" and "Historical Overview."

## PHOTOGRAPHERS

# INDEX

# PRAGUE

ISBN 3-88618-861-2

90000>

9 783886 188611

***Travel Destination***: Prague, the Beauty on the Vtlava, attracts millions of visitors. They climb to the castle and saunter along through the romantic alleys in the Lesser Town, visit the Charles Bridge and the Old Town Ring. Many of the splendid noble palaces, churches and monasteries of the city harbor interesting museums or are used as concert halls.

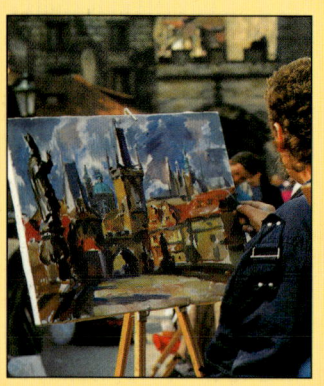

***Travel Information***: This Travel Guide recommends accommodation to fit every budget. It provides information on which pubs draw the best beer and which restaurants serve the best dumplings. Find out where the night-life pulses and where to buy Czech specialities. Many practical tips for the traveler are revealed in the handy chapter at the end of this book.